3230017459

WITHDRAWN

D0258525

Psychology and Health

Philippe Harari
Karen Legge

CARDONALD COLLEGE LIBRARY

L	613	H	3230017459
	019	A	
		R	

Heinemann Educational Publishers
Halley Court, Jordan Hill, Oxford, OX2 8EJ
a division of Reed Educational and Professional Publishing Ltd

OXFORD MELBOURNE AUCKLAND
JOHANNESBURG BLANTYRE GABORONE
IBADAN PORTSMOUTH (NH) USA CHICAGO

Heinemann is a registered trademark of Reed Educational and Professional Publishing Ltd

Text © Philippe Harari and Karen Legge, 2001

First published in 2001

05 04 03 02 01
10 9 8 7 6 5 4 3

All rights reserved

Apart from any fair dealing for the purposes of research or private study, or criticism or review as permitted under
the terms of the UK Copyright, Designs and Patents Act, 1988, this publication may not be reproduced, stored or
transmitted, in any form or by any means, without the prior permission in writing of the publishers, or in the case
of reprographic reproduction only in accordance with the terms of the licences issued by the Copyright Licensing
Agency in the UK, or in accordance with the terms of licences issued by the appropriate Reproduction Rights Organization outside the UK. Enquiries concerning reproduction outside the terms stated here should be sent to the
publishers at the address printed on this page.

British Library Cataloguing in Publication Data
A catalogue record for this book is available from the British Library

ISBN 0 435 80659 9

Typeset by Wyvern 21 Ltd
Picture research by Elaine Willis
Printed and bound in Great Britain by The Bath Press Ltd, Bath

Acknowledgements
The publishers would like to thank the following for permission to reproduce copyright material: *The Guardian* for
p. 40.

Cover photograph by AKG London

The publishers would like to thank the following for permission to use photographs: Associated Press, pp. 33 and
63; Horace Bristol/Corbis, p. 2; Science Photo Library, pp. 9, 22, 52, 72 and 88; Stock Market, pp. 22 and 53.

The publishers have made every effort to contact copyright holders. However, if any material has been incorrectly
acknowledged, the publishers would be pleased to correct this at the earliest opportunity.
Tel: 01865 888058 www.heinemann.co.uk

C Contents

Psychology and health

1 Introduction

Good health is very highly valued by almost all individuals and cultures but many people engage in activities that are downright damaging to their health. People spend a great deal of time and money trying to improve their health by different means, and at the same time ignoring factors that are causing them harm. Humanity has made great progress in terms of health care but there still remain many aspects of modern society that are harmful to people's well-being. The great contradiction of health is that a universal recognition of the importance and value of good health is accompanied by an apparent disregard for our own health and that of others. We live in an unhealthy world in which environmental damage, oppression and inequality, sickness and despair are prevalent. For many of us, goals such as material wealth, pleasure-seeking, power and influence and the search for knowledge seem very important, and the value of good health only becomes truly apparent when we fall ill.

As well as contradictions, the area of health also contains many controversies. People do not agree on how to improve health, or even on what health actually consists of. As a result, the task of improving health in our society is a multi-disciplinary one: advances in medical science are very important, but so are psychological treatments, public health initiatives, health education and health promotion programmes, and political changes aimed at reducing poverty, deprivation and conflict. Science, education, politics, philosophy and spiritual teaching can all contribute to a healthier world. Different people focus on different aspects, depending on their skills and ideological positions, but an understanding of psychology is useful to anybody working to improve people's health. Good psychology is all about improving people's well-being by developing and applying an understanding of human behaviour; health psychology focuses specifically on the aspects of human behaviour, thoughts and feelings that relate to physical well-being.

This book is a brief review of health psychology; it does not claim to be a comprehensive review of the topic, but it does attempt to introduce the reader to ways in which the study of psychology can be used to improve the state of people's health.

Chapter 1

This chapter describes two approaches to health that reflect different ways of defining what health means (the medical model and the biopsychosocial model), and looks at the role that health psychology has in understanding illness and health. It also examines a range of psychological theories (for example, behaviourist learning theories and cognitive theories such as the Health Belief Model) that explain health-related behaviours. The final section looks at cultural factors that can affect health (such as ethnicity).

Chapter 2

This chapter examines models of health promotion, including the way in which health messages can be communicated effectively to their target audience (for example, the Yale Model of Communication), and uses examples of workplace and school campaigns. It also applies psychological theories to an understanding of exercise and nutrition. Additionally, the chapter examines why people misuse substances and looks at addiction. This section also addresses ways of preventing and treating substance misuse (behavioural and cognitive). Finally, the chapter looks at psychological issues relating to health and safety, such as personality and accident proneness.

Chapter 3

This chapter looks at the way in which patients use medical services, particularly in relation to their adherence to medical advice, and their relationships with doctors. It looks at ways of measuring adherence, such as physical, self-report and observational measures, and the reasons why people do not adhere. The chapter also focuses on ways in which patients can be encouraged to adhere to the advice given to them, using advice and support groups. Finally, the chapter examines the difficulties that both patients and doctors face in communicating effectively with each other, both in terms of verbal and non-verbal communication.

Chapter 4

This chapter looks at the specific health-related issues of pain and stress. It examines these conditions in detail, and focuses on ways of measuring stress and pain (such as physiological, self-report and behavioural measures). It also describes and evaluates ways of managing and controlling these conditions (such as physical, cognitive and behavioural strategies). Additionally, the chapter looks at examples of chronic and terminal illnesses, and examines psychological factors affecting people with these illnesses.

How to use this book

This book has a number of features to help you understand the topic more easily. It is written to give you a wide range of skills in preparation for any of the new AS and A level psychology syllabi. Below is a list of the features with a brief summary to explain how to use them.

1 Real Life Applications

These consist of 'text boxes' that develop further a concept already discussed within the main text. Often they provide articles or outlines of studies. In all cases they attempt to apply theory to 'real life situations'.

2 Commentary

These paragraphs appear throughout the book. They follow on from issues raised within the main text. They serve a number of functions: to provide an evaluation of the earlier text, to clarify a point or to highlight some related issue. Sometimes they provide 'for' and 'against' debates.

3 Key studies

As the title implies these are descriptions of important studies within a specific area. There are two of these in each chapter. They briefly identify the aims, method, results and conclusions of the study. This feature helps you to understand the methodology of research.

4 Questions

Each 'Real Life Application' has between one and four short answer questions, designed to test a range of skills including summarising, outlining and evaluating. All of these activities are designed to allow you to acquire the 'key skills' outlined within the syllabi. In addition, a selection of 'essay-style' questions is included at the end of each chapter. They relate specifically to the material covered within that chapter.

5 Advice on answering questions

At the end of the book there is a short section that gives advice on answering the essay and short answer questions.

1 Factors affecting health

This chapter describes different models of health that reflect different ways of defining what health means, and looks at the important role that health psychology has in understanding illness and health. It also examines different psychological theories that explain health-related behaviours, and looks at cultural factors (such as ethnicity) that can affect health. Real Life Applications that are considered are:

- RLA 1: The Broad Street pump
- RLA 2: Anorexia nervosa

The psychology of health

Human beings have always spent a great deal of time and effort attempting to improve their own health and that of others. In our society, the medical profession is at the forefront of these attempts, but many other professions are also involved – public health workers, practitioners of complementary medicine and health psychologists, among others. In order to understand how to improve people's health, and the role that psychologists can play in this, it is first necessary to clarify what we mean by the concept of 'health' and to develop an understanding of the factors that contribute to it.

What is health?

The word 'health' is derived from the same root as 'whole', reflecting the traditional idea that a healthy person is someone who exists in a state of equilibrium of mind, body and spirit; when this equilibrium is disturbed, then the health of the individual is impaired.

This traditional idea of health underpins so-called 'alternative medicine'; **holistic** disciplines such as **acupuncture** or **ayurvedic medicine** use a variety of techniques to correct imbalances in the body. A central aspect of this traditional view is that healthiness is seen as a positive characteristic that an individual can possess to a greater or lesser degree. However, the concept of 'equilibrium of mind, body and spirit' is considered by many people as too vague, and the growth of professional medicine, which started about 200 years ago, resulted in changes in this attitude to health.

The medical model of health

Up until the end of the eighteenth century, health was perceived as a state positively characterized by certain qualities such as vigour, suppleness or fluidity. These qualities were lost or reduced as a result of illness, and the role of medicine was to restore them. As medicine came to be seen as more of a *science*, doctors established what the 'normal' functioning of the body should consist of and developed techniques aimed at bringing it back into normal working order. Doctors became less interested in whether patients *felt* unwell, but focused on **biological abnormalities** – diseases or injuries that could be observed objectively. As the biological mechanisms of human physiology became better understood by scientists, people started to perceive the body as a 'soft machine', operating according to the laws of physics. According to the medical model of health, healthiness occurs when the machine is in good working order. Ill health, therefore, is when parts of the machine start going wrong; just as a car is taken to be fixed by a qualified mechanic when it breaks down, so when the body goes wrong we go to a qualified doctor. The doctor will **diagnose** the problem (that is, determine which part of the machine is not working properly) and, if possible, either fix it or replace it.

Commentary

- The medical model is **reductionist**. Not only does it assume that the root cause of ill health is physiological, but also it tends to restrict its focus to the specific area of the body that is 'malfunctioning'. For example, a patient with eczema who visits a GP is likely to be prescribed some kind of steroid cream to make the rash go away. A more holistic approach may examine the role that stress plays in exacerbating the eczema, for example, and may aim its treatment at the immune system as a whole.

- The medical model is very much built around the concept of **biological normality** – that is, a person is healthy if his or her body is in 'normal' working order. However, this idea is questionable; for example, the effects of old age can be disabling and can lead an individual to experience unpleasant symptoms. But these effects are 'normal' and should not be classified as signs of a 'disease' according to the medical model, even though medical intervention is used to alleviate them (for example, using hormone replacement therapy). On the other hand, visual impairment, for example, is not biologically normal, but blind people may well consider themselves perfectly healthy, despite their poor eyesight.

- From a **scientific** perspective, evidence is only valid if it can be observed objectively. In a medical context, this means that a person is unhealthy if medical professionals are able to observe objective signs of disease or injury, whether the person feels ill or not. If an individual feels ill but there are no objective signs of disease, then the medical model would suggest that he or she is malingering (that is, pretending to be ill).

  A more **individualistic** approach would be to say that if a person feels ill – in other words perceives pain, discomfort or disability – then this is evidence enough to accept that he or she is unhealthy. For this

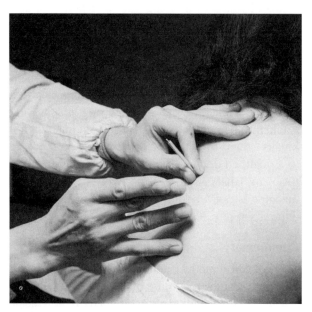

Acupuncture is a holistic discipline, which treats the whole person; traditional ideas of health are at the root of this form of complementary, or alternative, medicine.

definition to work, the subjective feeling of illness must be unpleasant and unwanted, but this leads to a contradiction; the pain associated with childbirth or the effects of extreme short-sightedness, for example, are unpleasant and may be unwanted, but most people would not see these as symptoms of ill health.

On the other hand, the refusal of doctors on occasions to accept that there is anything wrong with a patient just because they cannot detect any sign of disease or injury, and to ignore the patient's subjective report, can lead to patients being denied the treatment they need.

- Finally, in only considering the absence of disease or injury as a definition of health and ignoring positive characteristics, such as fitness or peace of mind, the medical model offers an incomplete picture; two individuals, both completely free of disease or injury at a particular moment in time, cannot be considered to be equally healthy.

The biopsychosocial model of health

In 1946, the World Health Organization wrote in its constitution that:

Health is … a state of complete physical, mental and social well-being and … not merely the absence of disease and infirmity.

This statement challenges the medical model in that it defines health as a positive state of well-being, and that it takes mental and social well-being into account as well as physical well-being. However, it implies that to be healthy, an individual needs to be in a state of 'complete' well-being, which is clearly impossible. Furthermore, it does not really explain what is meant by 'physical, mental and social well-being'.

The first problem is easily dealt with; a person's state of health lies along a continuum – the more physical, mental and social well-being an individual has, then the healthier he or she is. The second problem is more tricky. For example, it is necessary to distinguish between subjective well-being (a heroin user may feel really well while actually harming him or herself physically and psychologically) and 'true' well-being. Well-being is more than just feeling good, but it is difficult to come up with an objective definition with which everyone can agree.

One health psychologist, David Seedhouse (1986), argues that approaches to improving health have always tried to remove 'obstacles to the achievement potential'. These obstacles may be **biological** (for example, a flu virus that makes you feel too ill to go to work), **environmental** (for example, having to spend a large proportion of your time walking to a well to fetch clean water), **societal** (for example, being too poor to afford a proper diet), **familial** (for example, being the victim of abuse within the family), or **personal** (for example, not having the self-confidence or willpower to stop using drugs).

Seedhouse defines health as 'the set of conditions which fulfils or enables a person to work to fulfil his/her realistic chosen and biological potential' (1986, p. 61). In other words, physical, mental and social well-being means being able to achieve realistic goals set by yourself. For example, a student who performs badly in an exam because of a sore throat and headache is suffering from lowered **physical well-being**; if s/he does badly because of a panic attack, then that represents a lack of **mental well-being**; if s/he is unable to revise properly because of interruptions at home, then s/he has a lack of **social well-being**. On the other hand, a visually impaired person who has come to terms with the condition and is able to fulfil his or her potential within the physical constraints of the impairment would not be considered 'unhealthy' just because s/he cannot see very well.

Seedhouse's definition of health given above is still a bit vague, but, in simple terms, healthier people are more able to do what they want because they have fewer constraints. These constraints can occur within our **biological systems** (that is, our cells, tissues and organs), our **psychological systems** (that is, our cognitions, motivations and emotions) or our **social systems** (that is, our family and friends, our community and society).

Commentary

The **biopsychosocial** approach to health is holistic because it is interested in the *interaction* between the biological, psychological and social systems described above. It recognizes that no system exists in isolation and that an intervention at one level can have knock-on effects at other levels. For example, a certain psychological treatment such as cognitive therapy for stress may have an effect on a person's biological systems (for example, fewer headaches) and also on the social systems (for example, better family relationships). On the other hand, an approach that only focuses on one system is **reductionist**. The **medical model**, for example, only takes biological systems into account; Sigmund Freud (see page 4), on the other hand, tended to attribute physical symptoms to psychological factors alone and ignored possible physical causes.

The role of health psychology?

Health psychology has only been established as a separate discipline fairly recently, but doctors, scientists, psychologists and philosophers have debated the relationship between physical health and mental states for generations: this debate is often referred to as the **mind–body problem**.

The relationship between mind and body

One solution to the mind–body problem is to assume that all our experiences, including mental ones, are purely physical. In other words, our thoughts and emotions can be completely explained in terms of physiological brain processes. This approach sees the mind as a complicated machine capable, in theory, of replication in mechanical or electronic form. Extreme believers in this model would argue that one day we will be able to construct a machine that not only mimics the human body, but also the human mind.

At the other extreme, some philosophers have argued that all experiences, including physical ones, are purely mental. This approach argues that everything that we see, hear, smell and touch is known to us merely as internal sensations. In other words, our experience of the world occurs inside our own minds and may well have no objective reality of its own.

Both these approaches are **monistic** in that they argue that the mind and the body are indivisible, and that the well-being of one is impossible if the other is harmed or damaged. Most ancient health care systems (for example, traditional acupuncture and ayurvedic medicine) assume that good health comes from maintaining a balance between our minds, our bodies and the world around us. If we are is physically ill then it is hard to attain peace of mind and, on the other hand, a healthy state of mind is critical to the healing of physical ailments.

As the practice of physical medicine grew during the seventeenth century and the medical model of health became widely accepted, the idea that the mind and the body were the same, and could influence each other so closely, came to be seen as 'unscientific'. The French philosopher René Descartes (1596–1650) suggested the **dualistic** idea that mind and body both exist separately; the mind, or *soul*, 'lives within' the physical body. Most dualistic approaches accept that there must be an interaction between the mind and body (otherwise, how could the mind tell the body what to do).

However, they fail to explain properly how a

physical, material object (the body) can interact with a spiritual non-material entity (the mind); although Descartes suggested that this was through the **pineal gland** located at the front of the mid-brain. Descartes' dualistic solution to the mind–body problem has underpinned the medical model of health ever since as it views the body as a purely physical entity; ill health means that there is some physical damage to the body, and this needs to be repaired using mechanistic interventions. Although such interventions (for example, antibiotics or surgery) have been very successful in curing people from disease, it could be argued that the medical model has gone too far in concentrating on biological causes of disease and ignoring psychosocial factors.

Modern approaches to the mind-body problem

A serious challenge to the dualistic approach appeared during the twentieth century with an increasing number of doctors suggesting that psychological factors could effect physical ailments. The most famous of these was Sigmund Freud (1856–1939) who suggested that unresolved mental conflicts (such as feelings of guilt) are sometimes dealt with by suppressing them into the unconscious mind from which they later emerge in the form of physical symptoms: he called this process **conversion hysteria**. He treated a number of patients with physical symptoms using psychoanalysis to make them aware of their unconscious desires and conflicts. In fact, Freud has been criticized for ignoring possible physical causes for these symptoms and preventing some of his patients from receiving the medical treatment that would have cured them (for further details of some of these cases see Webster, 1996).

However, following the work of Freud and his disciples, most doctors began to accept that psychological factors could be very influential in physical conditions, even if their treatments still largely focused on the biological systems.

During the First World War, many soldiers displayed particular symptoms labelled **shellshock**. The panic attacks, flashbacks and so on associated with this condition are nowadays referred to as **Post-Traumatic Stress Disorder**, but shellshock provided doctors at the time with clear cases of physical illness seemingly unrelated to physiological causes. These cases may have contributed in the 1930s to the development of **psychosomatic medi-cine**, which recognized the relationship between certain conditions (for example, ulcers, high blood pressure) and mental states, such as stress or depression.

This relationship was accepted as a result of scientific experiments that provided evidence that emotions and cognitions could effect physiological responses. More recently, the role of the environment in affecting health has been recognized, again as the result of scientific experiments. **Behavioural medicine** tries to improve health by modifying behaviour. In the late 1970s, the new discipline of **health psychology** emerged, and has been growing in influence ever since. Health psychology recognizes that the physical body does not exist in isolation, and that there is a strong relationship between states of mind and health. Health psychologists attempt to discover the nature of this relationship, and use this knowledge to improve people's health.

The practice of health psychology

Health psychology has five main goals, as follows:

1 To prevent illness: health psychologists have argued strongly that it is better to prevent an illness than to cure it once it has occurred. Not only is this cheaper in the long run, but also it is also better for the 'patient'. The role of psychologists in preventing illness is to develop an understanding of how mental states can influence health behaviour. In other words, if we wish to stop people doing things that are bad for their health, we have to understand why they do those things in the first place.

2 To promote good health: because health psychologists see health as being more than just the absence of disease, they are interested in actively promoting well-being. A medical scientist may lose interest in a patient once his or her body has been restored to good working order, but a health psychologist would suggest that it is always possible to increase your level of physical and mental well-being.

3 To help with the treatment of illness: despite preventive measures, people do fall ill, and health psychologists have a role in developing treatments that take psychological aspects into account. For example, a doctor may treat a heart patient using drugs or surgery, but a health psychologist could contribute to the treatment by introducing a stress management programme.

4 To investigate the psychological correlates of illness: this is a vital aspect of the work of health psychologists. It involves carrying out research to find out which specific mental states are linked to which physical diseases. For example, the knowledge that stress is linked to high blood pressure can enable practitioners to identify people at risk as early as possible.

5 To improve the health care system and health policy: the knowledge gained by health psychologists, and their general approach to health and illness, can inform the people who run health care systems and help them to provide a more effective service.

This book will focus on the first three areas mentioned above – that is, preventing and treating illness, and promoting health. The next section describes different ways in which people's health can be improved.

Improving health

Perhaps the approach to improving health that most people think of first is the development of medical techniques. Over the past 300 years there has been a great deal of progress in medical science to the point where the causes of most diseases are understood and effective ways of treating them have been developed.

Doctors have a vast range of different drugs and surgical techniques at their disposal in the fight against disease. There still remain certain diseases that are considered 'untreatable', but advances in medical science have been accompanied by dramatic increases in life expectancy. We now live longer and healthier lives than ever before.

However, improvements in health have not just been as a result of more sophisticated medical practice. Perhaps the greatest single 'discovery' to contribute to increased life expectancy over the last 200 years has been proper sanitation. The impact of clean water and safe sewage disposal cannot be overestimated. Other **environmental** factors, such as war, famine and pollution, also play a significant role in people's health. The single factor that correlates most strongly with ill health is **poverty**. In the UK, people at the lower end of the socioeconomic scale have shorter, less healthy lives than people at the upper end (see pages 22–3). It could be argued that the most effective way of improving a nation's health is to reduce poverty, but this is easier said

than done. There are people living on the 'breadline' even in the most affluent countries in the world.

It is often easier and cheaper for governments to urge individuals to lead healthier lifestyles instead of spending public money improving the environment or tackling poverty. Behaviour change in individuals can be brought about through a combination of instruction (that is, telling people what to do in order to stay healthy), education (that is, providing people with knowledge and skills so that they can make informed health choices) and empowerment (that is, helping people develop the desire and the confidence to change). These three approaches to improving health – advances in medical science, behaviour change (through instruction, education and empowerment) and social change – are discussed in more detail in Chapter 2 (see page 26), and the relationship between them is illustrated in RLA 1.

Real Life Application 1:
The Broad Street pump

Cholera is a potentially fatal disease that is transmitted to humans through waterborne bacteria. In the first half of the nineteenth century medical practitioners did not know what caused cholera, nor how to treat it (antibiotics had not yet been discovered), and cholera epidemics were responsible for a great number of deaths. Various theories about the causes of cholera had been proposed; one theory blamed the disease on a fungus and another believed that miasma, or bad air, was responsible. This second theory probably arose from observing a high incidence of cholera in slum dwellings, where the air inside the houses was often very poor, especially in the winter, and a treatment was developed that consisted of sitting feverish cholera patients in front of open windows in the hope that the cold, fresh air would cure them.

John Snow (1813–1858) was an epidemiologist (that is, someone who investigates where and when cases of an illness occur, in the hope of spotting some kind of pattern that may point to an explanation) who believed that cholera was caused by some kind of germ passed from person to person via food or water polluted by sewage. In Snow's case, this theory was completely intuitive; he had no medical evidence to support it and was treated as irrational by his contemporaries. During the third cholera epidemic of 1854, Snow marked every new cholera case on a map of London. He noticed that almost all the cases were centred around a drinking water pump in Broad Street, Soho, with a few isolated cases in Hampstead and Islington (which, at the time, were villages outside of London) (see fig. 1.1). Snow discovered that a 'Hampstead widow' had developed a taste for the water from the Broad Street pump and received regular bottles of it from relatives living in the area. A niece of hers, who lived in an area with no cholera but visited her aunt regularly and drank the Broad Street water, also died of the disease.

Despite this evidence, the Committee of Scientific Enquiries did not accept that the Broad Street pump was directly responsible for the current cholera epidemic, probably because of the absence of any direct medical evidence and because it contradicted other people's theories of how cholera was spread. In the light of this rejection, Snow's efforts to persuade the people living near Broad Street to stop using the pump failed; they could not see how water could make you ill, and it was too much effort to travel further afield to collect water. Having failed to persuade the medical profession that cholera was carried by waterborne germs, and the people of Soho to change their behaviour, John Snow actually stole the handle from the Broad Street pump to prevent people from using it. As a result of this action, the cholera epidemic ended.

This historical incident illustrates how medical knowledge is not necessary in order to understand how to improve prevent disease; it also shows how direct environmental action can be much more effective in protecting people's health than trying to persuade them to change their lifestyles.

Adapted from *Cholera, fever and English medicine* by Margaret Pelling, 1978.

Summary

- By plotting the incidence of cholera cases in London in 1854, John Snow discovered that the disease was caused by drinking contaminated water.
- Having failed to convince either the medical profession or the general public that the water was unsafe to drink, Snow took matters into his own hands and removed the Broad Street pump handle, thereby ending that particular cholera epidemic.

Questions

1 What is epidemiology and how can it help with the promotion of health?

2 Health can be promoted by advances in medical science, behavioural changes and environmental improvements. Which technique did Snow use, and why?

3 In removing the pump handle, Snow was ignoring the wishes of the local population; was he morally right to do this?

Health-related behaviour

The previous section mentions the three ways in which health promotion can occur – that is:

- advances in medical science
- behavioural changes
- social change.

Medical science is the province of doctors and biochemists, social change is brought about through political activity, but it is behavioural change that is of interest to health psychologists; the study of psychology helps us to understand the factors that influence human behaviour, and by understanding behaviour, we may be able to change it. This section starts by defining the concept of health-related behaviour, then goes on to describe five different types of theory that attempt to explain why some people lead healthier lives than others:

- genetic theories
- behaviourist learning theories
- social and environmental factors
- emotional factors
- cognitive theories.

The notion that an individual's health can be improved by a change in behaviour is based on the assumption that certain specific behaviours or lifestyles are better for health than others. This seems a safe assumption; it is clear that certain behaviours, such as smoking tobacco for example, can lead directly to specific medical conditions. It is also generally accepted that overall lifestyle can affect health; a person who leads a hectic, stressful life is more likely to develop high blood pressure or coronary heart disease, for example.

Specific behaviours can increase or reduce the risk of becoming ill in the first place, but individual behaviour can also effect the chances of recovery

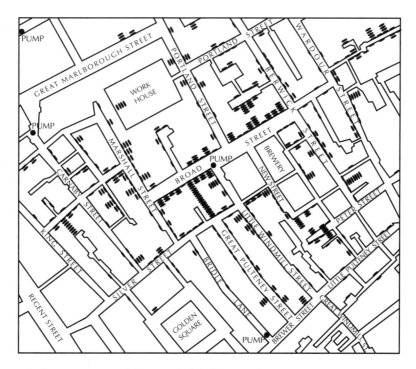

Figure 1.1: A portion of John Snow's map of the spread of cholera in Soho.
Reprinted from *Health Promotions: Foundation for Practice 2/e*, J Naidoo and J. Wills, figure 9.1, p. 185, ©2000, by permission of the publisher Ballière Tindall.

from disease or injury. For example, recognizing the early signs of an illness and seeking medical help is a behaviour that promotes health.

Pitts defines **preventive health behaviours** as 'behaviours undertaken by people to enhance or maintain their health' (1996, p. 3). She quotes a study by Belloc and Breslow (1972) in which they asked a sample of 6928 residents of Alameda County, California, which of a list of seven preventive health behaviours they practised regularly (for example, not smoking, drinking alcohol in moderation, taking regular exercise). They also asked participants about the state of their physical, mental and social health (that is, how well they functioned in their community).

The results showed that people who carried out more preventive health behaviours were actually healthier. Follow-up studies ten, seventeen and twenty-five years later showed that people who had got into the habit of practising all seven health behaviours had lower mortality rates (that is, lived longer).

Commentary

- There are several methodological criticisms that can be made of the original study by Belloc and Breslow and the follow-up studies. First, the sample is not par-

ticularly representative as all the participants came from the same area in the USA. Second, the study establishes a correlation between seven specific health preventive behaviours and longevity, but does not prove that these behaviours actually caused some of the participants to live longer. It is possible, although unlikely, that some other factor – personality, for example – affected both behaviour and lifespan.

- The 'behavioural change' approach to promoting health raises a couple of ethical issues. First, it can lead to 'victim-blaming'. If we believe too strongly that individuals can prevent themselves from falling ill by choosing to carry out health preventive behaviours, then we may go on to blame those individuals for failing to protect their own health if they do fall ill.

There have been cases where doctors have refused to treat certain patients because they felt that they had brought their illnesses on themselves. As mentioned earlier (see pages 5–6) the greatest contributions to health have been through developments in medical science and through public health initiatives such as improved sanitation, and not through individual behavioural change. The question of how we attribute our ill health is discussed in the section on health locus of control (see pages 15–16).

The second problem with the behavioural change approach is the narrow line that exists between persuading someone to change his or her behaviour and coercion. Do we have a right to assume that we know better than someone else what is best for their own health, and to force them to change their behaviour accordingly (for example, was John Snow right to steal the handle of the Broad Street pump? See RLA 1, page 5).

Genetic theories

Genetics has an obvious impact on people's health in the sense that many diseases have genetic components. It is rarely the case that an individual's genetic inheritance actually determines his or her state of health, rather that some people are born with a genetic disposition towards certain conditions. Such people are more likely than others to develop a particular condition, but whether they actually do or not depends on environmental and behavioural factors.

It is possible for genetic disposition towards a particular condition to have an indirect impact on health preventive behaviour. For example, a woman whose mother and grandmother had breast cancer may be more likely to examine her own breasts for lumps because she feels that she is more susceptible to the disease than average.

Is it possible, however, for a person's genetic inheritance to directly affect their health-related behaviour? It may be, for example, that alcoholism is partly hereditary. In his book on this topic, Sher (1991) describes evidence that the children of alcoholics are more likely to become alcoholic themselves.

Although it is notoriously difficult to determine whether a correlation such as this is due to genetic factors or arises as a result of social learning, some psychologists argue that, although there probably is no such thing as an 'alcoholism gene', certain genetically inherited personality traits may pre-dispose an individual towards alcohol abuse.

The link between genes and alcoholism may be even more subtle. Richard Burton, the famous actor, was once quoted as saying that he would never have become an alcoholic if he had ever suffered a hangover. The ability to drink heavily without getting a headache the following morning may well be linked to the way the body metabolizes alcohol, and this may be partly affected by genetic inheritance (see RLA 5 in Chapter 2, page 40).

Commentary

Among all the theories described in this chapter, this is the only one that comes down firmly on the 'nature' side of the nature-nurture debate. All the others explain difference in behaviour between individuals in terms of social or environmental influences. However, even the most hard-line biopsychologist would accept that health-related behaviour is not completely determined by genetic inheritance; the most that genetics can do is to pre-dispose an individual towards a particular behaviour.

Behaviourist learning theories

Classical conditioning is a process in which the individual associates an automatic response with a neutral stimulus. Ivan Pavlov (1849–1936) described this process after he noticed that laboratory dogs would salivate when he turned a light on because they had learnt to associate the light with the presence of food.

Classical conditioning could explain certain health-related behaviours such as 'comfort eating', for example. If a parent regularly offers a child sweets or chocolate at the same time as physical and emotional affection, then the child may learn to associate sweet foods with the reassuring feelings that arise out of parental love. In later life, the child may try to recreate these pleasant feelings by eating chocolate when he or she is stressed or depressed.

Another example of how classical conditioning could effect health behaviour is based on the concept of **one-trial learning**. Pavlov noticed that some of his dogs developed a phobia of water following an incident in which the basement they were kept in flooded and they nearly drowned. In the same way, a single frightening or painful visit to a dentist, for example, could create an irrational fear of dentists, leading to avoidance.

Operant conditioning is when people respond to reward or punishment by either repeating a particular behaviour, or else stopping it. If an individual carries out a behaviour that clearly seems to be bad for his or her health, such as smoking cigarettes, a deeper look may well reveal benefits for the individual, such as social approval, the nicotine buzz and so on.

A striking example of how operant conditioning can effect health behaviour is the study by Gil *et al* (1988). They conducted research on children suffering from a chronic skin disorder that causes severe itching. They videotaped the children with their parents in the hospital and observed that when parents tried to stop their children scratching (in order to prevent peeling and infection) this actually increased the scratching behaviour by rewarding it with attention. When they asked parents to ignore their children when they scratched and give them positive attention when they did not scratch, the amount of scratching was significantly reduced.

Any attempt to get people to change their health behaviour by offering inducements, or threatening punishments or penalties, is based on the principle of operant conditioning, and this is revisited in other places in this book.

Social learning occurs when an individual observes and imitates another person's behaviour, either because the individual looks up to that person as a role model or else through **vicarious reinforcement** – that is, the individual sees the person being rewarded for his or her actions. A study that illustrates this process was carried out by Albert Bandura (1965); he showed three groups of children videotapes of a man being aggressive towards a doll. One group saw the man being rewarded for his aggression, the second group saw him being punished and the third were not shown any consequences at all. When the children were put into a room with a smaller doll and observed, the group who had seen the model being rewarded imitated significantly more of the aggressive behaviour than the other two groups.

Social learning can clearly be very influential in encouraging people to do things that are bad for their health (for example, a teenager may take up smoking because he or she has an admired elder brother who smokes, or may try illegal drugs because he or she sees other people taking them and having a good time).

Another example of how vicarious reinforcement can lead to unhealthy behaviour concerns young women with eating disorders, who see images of very thin models in magazines being rewarded with success, money, glamour and fame (see RLA 2, page 17). On the other hand, many health promotion campaigns use positive role models to try to get people to lead healthier lifestyles. The advertising industry, whose reason for existing is to persuade people to change their behaviour, often depicts successful, good-looking and happy people using a certain product in the hope that this will make others want to use the product as well. This technique for persuading people to change their behaviour will be examined in more detail in Chapter 2 in the section on health promotion (see pages 26–7).

Commentary

Many psychologists criticize behaviourist learning theories on the grounds that they are too **mechanistic**. In other words, they assume that human beings respond automatically to specific situations. Not only does this imply a lack of free will, but also it also ignores the effect on behaviour of **cognitive** factors. It seems reasonable to assume that our attitudes and opinions have a significant effect on our behaviour, and that one way to modify behaviour is to change people's attitudes; this is discussed later in this chapter in the section on cognitive theories (see pages 11–18).

Social and environmental factors

There are many different social and environmental factors contributing to people's health behaviour. For example, a common explanation for young people taking drugs or smoking cigarettes is 'peer pressure'. It may be that people imitate their peers because of the explanation given above – that is, vicarious reinforcement; they see others getting a reward for a certain behaviour, so they copy it.

A different psychological concept that can explain how peer pressure works is **conformity** in which people act the same as members of their own social group in order to fit in, to gain social acceptance or to reinforce their social identity. In his classic study

Peer group pressure can be a strong force in persuading individuals to behave in the same way as other members of a group.

on conformity, Solomon Asch (1956) asked male college students to take part in an experiment about 'visual judgement' that involved looking at a line and saying which of three other lines it was closest to in length. In fact, the correct response was obvious, but the participant had to make the judgement after several confederates deliberately gave the wrong answer. Asch found that 70% of his participants conformed on at least one occasion by giving the wrong answer themselves.

Asch's study shows how people will deny the evidence of their own eyes in order to fit in with a group of people they had never even met before. In situations where the decision is a little more ambiguous, and the peer group is known to the individual, conformity is likely to be an even more powerful influence. For example, if someone goes to the pub with a group of friends, there is likely to be pressure put on that person to drink alcohol. If he or she does not drink, for religious reasons say, then the situation is unambiguous and it is easier to resist the social influence. If, on the other hand, the person has decided not to drink just for that evening, and is worried about being excluded from the social group if he or she does not join in, the pressure to have a drink could be almost irresistible.

Commentary

- Conformity does not exert an equally strong influence in all situations and with all individuals. It is likely to be more powerful in ambiguous situations, when others are perceived as having more expertise, or when the individual has low self-confidence, poor self-esteem and a weak sense of self-efficacy (see page 15).
- Asch's study was carried out many years ago, on male participants only, and in the USA. It may be unwise to assume that the high levels of conformity observed by Asch would appear in a similar study carried out nowadays.

Emotional factors

There are obvious ways in which an individual's emotional state could effect his or her health behaviour; people who are stressed or depressed are more likely to smoke, drink, eat an unbalanced diet and have accidents, for example. This section, however, looks at the concept of **ego defence mechanisms**, described by Sigmund Freud.

Freud suggested that at times of anxiety or psychological tension we use a range of techniques that make us feel better by protecting us from negative emotions. These defence mechanisms work by distorting or denying reality; people make themselves feel better by avoiding their problems. The main defence mechanisms described by Freud are set out below, with examples showing how they can affect health behaviour.

- **Denial** is where people pretend to themselves that a certain event simply did not happen, or that a particular situation does not exist. An example of this would be an elderly man who literally cannot accept that his wife has died and keeps talking about her coming home. Denial such as this can go on for some time, until the individual feels psychologically ready to face reality. A health-related example of denial is when someone has a symptom that may indicate the onset of a life-threatening disease, such as cancer, and is so scared of accepting that he or she might be ill that he stops perceiving the symptom at all.

  Clearly, denial is an extreme form of avoidance and is fairly rare. Most people faced with such a situation would recognize the symptom but may use other defence mechanisms to stop themselves worrying about it.

- **Suppression** is where people deliberately and consciously try not to think about things that might upset them. They know that they have a worrying symptom, but they make efforts to distract themselves from even thinking about it. There are many techniques that can be used in suppression: going out with friends, watching television or simply giving oneself mental instructions not to think about something (although this is easier said than done).

- **Repression** also involves pushing thoughts out of the conscious mind, but in this case the process is unconscious. Examples of this are when someone has a doctor's appointment that he or she is dreading and forgets to go, or when people forget to take unpleasant medication.

In order to understand the distinction between denial, suppression and repression, imagine facing an individual with the information he or she is trying to avoid – possible evidence of skin cancer, for example. Someone who is trying to suppress the information may say, 'Yes, I know, but I'm trying not to think about it'; someone who is unconsciously repressing the information may say 'Oh, I'd forgotten all about that – it is quite worrying now that you mention it';

the person in denial would challenge the existence of the symptom: 'There's nothing there, I don't know what you're talking about.'

- **Rationalization** involves justifying or making excuses for an action in order to convince oneself that it is not so bad. For example, the teenager who watches a health promotion video about the dangers of tobacco and then says, 'I don't need to worry because I'm not as old as the people in the video, and I'll have given up smoking by the age of 25, and anyway I could get run over by a bus tomorrow' is using rationalization as a defence mechanism.

- **Displacement** is when someone has negative feelings towards something but is unable to express those feelings to the source so redirects them towards a safer target. For example, if a teenager is told off by his or her parents, is upset and resentful but does not feel able to argue back, he or she may well take it out on a younger brother or sister.

- **Projection** is when we have thoughts, feelings or behaviours that we consider unacceptable or that we are very ashamed about. Instead of criticizing ourselves, we unconsciously attribute these thoughts, feelings or behaviours to other people. For example, some people argue that many homophobic men are, in fact, uncertain about their own sexuality and are deeply ashamed at the thought that they may be gay, so they attack other gay people instead of coming to terms with their own internal conflicts.

Displacement and projection are less relevant to health behaviour than the other four types of defence mechanism mentioned above.

Commentary

- It seems clear that ego defence mechanisms are not the best way to deal with stressful or worrying situations. By avoiding a problem, the individual may well feel emotionally better in the short term, but the problem is unlikely to go away and, as mentioned earlier (see page 4) Freud argues that when we push mental conflicts into our unconscious mind in order to avoid them, they can actually lead directly to physical illness, not to mention long-term mental distress. The effectiveness of avoidance techniques will be discussed more fully in Chapter 4 in the section on managing and controlling stress (see pages 83–5).

Cognitive theories

People's cognitions, their beliefs, opinions, motivations and so on, clearly have an impact on their behaviour in general and their health behaviour in particular. It is often said, for example, that you cannot get someone to give up smoking or drugs unless that person wants to.

Traditional behaviourists, on the other hand, may argue that as long as a child is systematically being rewarded for a certain action, he or she will learn to continue with that action and his or her thought processes are completely irrelevant.

Cognitive psychologists would criticize this approach on the grounds that it ignores a key aspect of human nature; the ability to think things through and make rational decisions. They would argue that it is important to understand the cognitive determinants of behaviour because, by changing these, the behaviour itself can be modified. There is no single overarching cognitive theory to explain why and how people make health-related decisions, but a great deal of research has been carried out to investigate the impact of specific cognitive factors. To represent some of this research, this section examines four different, but related, theories that attempt to explain how our beliefs and opinions can affect our health behaviour:

- Health Belief Model
- Theory of Reasoned Action/Theory of Planned Behaviour
- Self-efficacy
- Locus of control

Health Belief Model

The Health Belief Model was initially developed as a theory in the 1950s to explain the widespread failure of people to take part in preventive health campaigns, such as the free tuberculosis screening programme introduced by the Public Health Service in the USA.

Hochbaum (1958) carried out research on 1200 adults living in cities that had recently introduced the tuberculosis screening programme. He identified two key factors in predicting behaviour: first, whether the people felt they were personally at risk of catching tuberculosis; and second, whether they believed that early detection and treatment would be effective. Some 80% of people who held both these beliefs went for screening, whereas only 20% who held neither of these beliefs went for screening.

This study shows that specific beliefs are highly

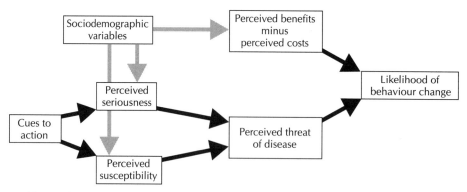

Figure 1.2: The Health Belief Model

correlated to particular health behaviours. The implications of this for health promotion are obvious: if we understand how health decisions are made and which specific beliefs are important in those decisions, then by persuading people to adopt certain beliefs, we can get them to change their behaviour. Following Hochbaum's survey, the Health Belief Model was developed and extended to cover all types of health behaviour, not just attending screening for tuberculosis (Strecher and Rosenstock, 1997).

The Health Belief Model is made up of the following components (see Figure 1.2).

- **Perceived threat of disease:** people would not even consider a health behaviour unless they saw some need for it – in other words, a key component of any health behaviour is the perception that the individual is at risk in the first place. Many health education or health promotion campaigns attempt to create the perception of risk by presenting information about how *serious* the threat is. Examples of this would include stories about people dying of lung or throat cancer as a result of smoking, or showing graphic images of the victims of drink-driving accidents.

   The effectiveness of this type of **fear arousal** is discussed more fully in Chapter 2 in the section on health promotion (see pages 26–7), but all that fear arousal on its own can do is make people realize that a particular condition is potentially serious; it cannot convince them that they are personally at risk.

   For example, all young smokers recognize that smoking can cause lung cancer and that lung cancer is a very serious disease, but this does not necessarily mean that they feel their own chances of getting lung cancer are particularly high. By using a process of rationalization (see page 11), for example, they may convince themselves that they

are not personally at risk. Similarly, everyone knows that a single tablet of ecstasy can be fatal, but the chances of this are so very low that this probably puts very few people off taking the drug.

So, in order to convince individuals that there is a threat of disease (**perceived threat**), you have to convince them first that the disease is potentially serious (**perceived seriousness**) and second that they are individually at risk (**perceived susceptibility**).

- **Perceived benefits and barriers:** once an individual has accepted that there is a real threat, he or she will not change his or her behaviour unless s/he believes that this will actually reduce the threat. For example, if a woman believes that she is at high risk of breast cancer, and recognizes how serious an illness this is, she will not carry out breast self-examination unless she believes that this is an effective way to diagnose breast cancer and that it will lead to a cure. However, even if people do recognize the benefits of a certain health behaviour, the costs of this behaviour (in terms of time, money, inconvenience, discomfort and so on) may outweigh the potential benefits.

The Health Belief Model, then, predicts that individuals will undertake behaviour change if:

a they perceive a threat to their health

b the perceived benefits of the behaviour change outweigh the perceived barriers.

- **Cues to action:** in his original research, Hochbaum (1958) suggested that perceived threat of disease in an individual is triggered by cues to action. These include bodily events (such as the onset of symptoms) or environmental events (such as media publicity, magazine articles or seeing other people become ill). This idea has never been systematically studied, but it seems to make sense. For example, we can live a sedentary life quite happily until someone of our own age dies of heart disease, or we read an article or see a poster that makes us think about the fact that we are not taking enough exercise. If we then see that our lifestyle is unhealthy (perceived threat) and the benefits of taking more exercise seem to outweigh the costs, we may well decide to change our behaviour.

- **Sociodemographic variables:** the Health Belief Model recognizes that its key elements – perception of threat, and of the costs and benefits of a certain action – are affected by certain modifying factors such as age, gender, ethnicity and socioeconomic status (see pages 22–3), and our previous experience, education and knowledge. This means that two people may well perceive the same situation differently, depending on their backgrounds. The way that sociodemographic variables can affect the elements of the Health Belief Model is illustrated with the lighter coloured arrows in Figure 1.2 (see page 12).

Commentary

There are several criticisms that can be made of the Health Belief Model:

- Many studies similar to Hochbaum's have been carried out in order to provide support for the Health Belief Model and these have tended to find that **perceived cost** is the single most powerful predictor of behaviour, followed by **perceived susceptibility** and **perceived benefits**, and finally by **perceived seriousness** (Strecher and Rosenstock, 1997).

  This implies that the most effective way to change behaviour is to limit the barriers (that is, by making healthier choices easier choices), and the least effective is to try to convince people of the seriousness of the situation. The criticism of this research, however, is that it has tended to consider each of the elements of the Health Belief Model in isolation; very little research has been done that looks at how people with different combinations of health beliefs vary in their likelihood of carrying out health behaviours.

- The Health Belief Model is a decision-making model that describes how a person will arrive at the decision to change their behaviour. The best that it can do, therefore, is to predict the 'likelihood' of behaviour change; it is clear that behaviour change is more likely to occur if an individual has made the decision

to change, but this does not guarantee that the behaviour will occur. For example, a person may feel a sharp pain in his or her tooth (cue to action) and may perceive a health threat as a result of tooth decay. He or she may decide that the benefits of visiting the dentist outweigh the costs and, as a consequence, makes an appointment. However, it may be the case that this individual has a phobia of dentists (see page 8) and may fail to turn up to the appointment. The Health Belief Model is a purely cognitive theory, and does not take emotional or irrational factors into account.

- On the other hand, not all health behaviours arise out of a rational decision. For example, before brushing their teeth in the morning, how many people stop to decide whether they perceive seriousness and susceptibility, and weigh up the cost and benefits of the behaviour? Similarly, people can do things that are bad for their health – such as smoking, or eating too much chocolate – without really considering the consequences every time. Many health behaviours are done out of habit, and the Health Belief Model does not take this into account.

Theory of Reasoned Action/Theory of Planned Behaviour

The Theory of Planned Behaviour (Ajzen, 1991) is an extension of an earlier model, the Theory of Reasoned Action (Ajzen and Fishbein, 1980). The Theory of Reasoned Action assumes that people's behaviour is determined by their intentions; in other words, first we decide to do something, and then we do it. Intention to behave is determined by the following two factors.

- Attitude towards the behaviour is the individual's personal beliefs about the possible consequences of the behaviour. For example, if an individual believes that taking more exercise will be good for him or her, then s/he is more likely to take exercise. This component of the Theory of Reasoned Action is similar to the Health Belief Model in that it combines perceived threat and perceived costs and benefits into a single belief about how good a particular behaviour is for one's health.

- Subjective norm represents social influence (this is not considered by the Health Belief Model) and consists of the individual's beliefs about other people's attitudes to the behaviour. For example, a person may well take friends' or family members' opinions into account when deciding whether to give up smoking. If the individual perceives that his or her friends disapprove of smoking, and this matters to the individual, then he or she is more likely to decide to give up.

To sum up, the Theory of Reasoned Action says that intention to behave, and therefore actual behaviour, depends on:

a the perceived consequences of the behaviour
b the attitudes of significant other people.

In order to change behaviour, it is necessary to change these underlying beliefs.

The Theory of Planned Behaviour adds a third, very important, factor to the Theory of Reasoned Action.

Perceived behavioural control refers to how confident the individual is that he or she will succeed in changing their behaviour. If a person feels confident that s/he can give up smoking, for example, then s/he is more likely to decide to try. This belief, which is very similar to the notion of self-efficacy described below (see page 15), is based on past experiences and also on the individual's perception of possible obstacles that might crop up in the future.

Figure 1.3 shows how the different factors interact in the Theory of Planned Behaviour. Intention to behave determines actual behaviour and is itself determined by attitude towards the behaviour, subjective norm and perceived behavioural control. These three factors can influence each other – for example, other people's attitudes can influence the degree to which a person feels confident about behaviour change. Similarly, the degree of confidence a person feels about behaviour change can affect his or her beliefs about the consequences of the behaviour change. Furthermore, perceived behavioural control not only affects the intention to behave, but also can have a direct impact on whether the behaviour is actually carried out; someone with high perceived behavioural control is likely to try harder to convert his or her intention to behave into actual behaviour.

Commentary

- Both the Theory of Reasoned Action and the Theory of Planned Behaviour predict intention to behave and intention does not always lead to actual behaviour. Neither of these theories considers what happens between deciding to do something, and actually doing it. However, the link between intention and actual behaviour is likely to be stronger if:

  a the intention is very specific (that is, 'I have decided to limit myself to two halves of lager tonight' is more likely to lead to a change in behaviour than 'I have decided to cut down on my drinking')
  b there is a shorter time between the intention and the behaviour (a delay allows more opportunity for the individual to change his or her intention).

- As with the Health Belief Model, much research has been carried out to test the validity of the Theory of Reasoned Action and the Theory of Planned Behaviour (see Key Study 1, page 17 for an example of this kind of research). Sutton (1997), for example, says that the Theory of Reasoned Action seems to explain about 50% of variations in intention to behave between people, and about 25% of variations in actual behaviour. This means that the Theory of Reasoned Action is quite good at predicting intention to behave and actual behaviour, but does not tell the whole story. The Theory of Planned Behaviour includes an additional variable and is therefore better than the Theory of Reasoned Action at predicting behaviour but, again only tells part of the story.

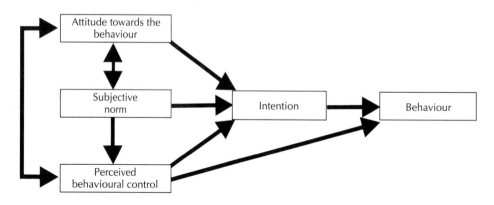

Figure 1.3: Theory of Planned Behaviour

Sutton states that although the theories are useful for prediction, they do not provide an accurate description of how people make health-related decisions.

Self-efficacy

In the Theory of Planned Behaviour, the notion of perceived behavioural control represents the individual's beliefs about his or her ability to carry out successfully a certain behaviour. Bandura (1986) refers to this concept as self-efficacy. Clearly, high levels of self-efficacy are likely to be linked to greater motivation to change behaviour; people who feel more confident that they can succeed are more likely to attempt health-related behaviour change and will show greater perseverance. In order to understand how it may be possible to foster a greater sense of self-efficacy in people, it is necessary to explore the factors that contribute to high or low levels of self-efficacy.

Bandura (1986) describes four different influences that can affect self-efficacy:

- **Enactive influences:** these refer to the individual's past experiences of success and failure. Someone who is used to being successful will feel more confident about succeeding in future, and vice versa. For example, a person who has tried to give up smoking on several occasions, and failed every time, may be less inclined to try again than someone who has not had this experience of failure.

- **Vicarious influences:** these consist of comparing oneself with others and judging our own competence accordingly (that is, 'If they can do it, then so can I'). One technique for improving people's self-efficacy is to present them with examples of people that they can identify with and who have been successful in carrying out a specific health behaviour. For example, it may well boost someone's confidence in his or her ability to give up smoking if s/he meets someone who used to smoke more than s/he does, and has successfully given up.

- **Persuasory influences:** Bandura suggests that an individual's self-efficacy can be enhanced by other people persuading him or her that they can successfully undertake the task in question. When it comes to health behaviours, this positive feedback can come from friends and family, from health professionals or even from health promotion materials.

- **Emotive influences:** Bandura suggests that over-anxiety may lead an individual to feel that he or she is not capable of succeeding at a specific task. For example, if someone has decided to cut down on drinking, but is anxious about the possible consequences, this anxiety may undermine the person's confidence in his or her ability to drink less.

Commentary

Much research seems to show that self-efficacy is one of the most important cognitive factors in influencing health behaviour (see Key Study 1, page 17). This implies that there is no point telling young people about the dangers of smoking or the importance of using condoms unless those people feel confident about their ability to give up smoking or to negotiate condom use with their partner. The notion that health promotion should focus more on providing people with the skills and confidence to change their behaviour, rather than simply telling them about the dangers of not changing their behaviour, will be discussed more fully in Chapter 2 in the sections on health promotion (see pages 26–7).

Locus of control

Ajzen (1991) believed that **self-efficacy** and **perceived behavioural control** are one and the same. However, Povey *et al* (2000) (see Key Study 1, page 17) argue that perceived behavioural control is made up of two components: one of these is Bandura's notion of self-efficacy; the other is **perceived control over the behaviour** – in other words, the extent to which the individual believes that the situation is under his or her control, or the extent to which he or she feels responsible for his/her own health. This second component is very similar to the notion of **locus of control** – that is, people's beliefs about whether what happens to them and what they do is under their own control (**internal**), or whether there is little that they can do to change things (**external**).

Wallston *et al* (1978) developed a scale specifically designed to measure the extent to which people perceive their state of health as being under internal or external control. Their Multidimensional Health Locus of Control Scale (MHLC) identifies three distinct ways in which people attribute their health status:

1 **Internal health locus of control (IHLC):** someone with a strong IHLC will feel responsible for his or her own health and will believe s/he can

improve his or her health by taking action. This means that s/he is more likely to blame themselves if s/he does fall ill, but then s/he is also more likely to try to lead a healthier life. There is quite a lot of research evidence to indicate that having an IHLC is good for your health.

2 **Powerful others health locus of control (PHLC):** this refers to the belief that other people are responsible for your state of health, either for the bad (for example, 'I only smoke because my friends make me') or for the good (for example, 'If I do what my doctor tells me, then I will stay healthy'). People with a strong PHLC are less likely to take personal responsibility for changing their own lifestyles, but are more likely to seek help from health professionals.

3 **Chance health locus of control (CHLC):** people with a strong CHLC tend to be fatalistic about their health (for example, 'There's nothing I can do about it; if I'm unlucky then I will get ill' or 'There's no point looking after my health; I might get run over by a bus tomorrow'). This group is the least likely to take responsibility for looking after their own health.

Figure 1.4 shows an example of Wallston *et al*'s (1978) MHLC scale. The number of IHLC, PHLC and CHLC items that an individual agrees with indicates how he or she tends to attribute health status.

Commentary

- Health attributions are not constant; they may vary with time and according to the specific issue that is being considered. For example, a person may feel responsible for the fact that he or she smokes (**internal**) but not for catching a cold virus from someone else (chance) or for being given the wrong medication by a doctor (**powerful others**). However, different individuals seem to have a tendency to attribute illness in particular ways. For example, out of three people who have all caught a cold, one may blame him or herself for not taking enough vitamins or dressing up warmly enough (**internal**), another may simply see it as bad luck (chance), and the third may actually blame the person who passed on the virus (**powerful others**).

- If it is true that people who tend to attribute health internally end up being healthier, then it may be productive to look at ways for modifying people's locus

of control, either by carrying out research into why people develop specific attribution styles, or by developing forms of treatment that can help people feel more in control of what happens to them.

The study by Povey *et al* (2000) (see Key Study 1, page 17) is an example of research aimed at discovering which cognitive factors are most influential in determining health behaviour. This is followed by RLA 2 (see page 17), which describes different types of explanation for a specific condition, anorexia nervosa.

The statements given below are taken from the paper written by Wallston *et al* (1978). Respondents could be asked to rate each statement on a 5-point Lickert scale according to how much they agree with them.

Statements 1, 6, 8, 12, 13, 17 measure internal health locus of control (IHLC)

Statements 3, 5, 7, 10, 14, 18 measure powerful others health locus of control (PHLC)

Statements 2, 4, 9, 11, 15, 16 measure chance health locus of control (CHLC)

1 If I get sick, it is my own behaviour which determines how soon I get well again.
2 No matter what I do, if I am going to get sick, I will get sick.
3 Having regular contact with my physician is the best way for me to avoid illness.
4 Most things that affect my health happen to me by accident.
5 Whenever I don't feel well, I should consult a medically trained professional.
6 I am in control of my health.
7 My family has a lot to do with my becoming sick or staying healthy.
8 When I get sick I am to blame.
9 Luck plays a big part in determining how soon I will recover from an illness.
10 Health professionals control my health.
11 My good health is largely a matter of good fortune.
12 The main thing which affects my health is what I myself do.
13 If I take care of myself, I can avoid illness.
14 When I recover from an illness, it's usually because other people (for example, doctors, nurses, family, friends) have been taking good care of me.
15 No matter what I do, I'm likely to get sick.
16 If it's meant to be, I will stay healthy.
17 If I take the right actions, I can stay healthy.
18 Regarding my health, I can only do what my doctor tells me to do.

Figure 1.4: The Multidimensional Health Locus of Control Scale (MHLC)

KEY STUDY 1

Researchers: Povey *et al* (2000)

Aim: To examine the application of the Theory of Planned Behaviour to two particular dietary behaviours – cutting down on fatty food, and eating five portions of fruit and vegetables per day. The study looks at a specific component of the Theory of Planned Behaviour – perceived behavioural control, which Povey et al argue is made up of self-efficacy and locus of control.

Method: Some 390 people responded to an advert placed in a regional newspaper asking for volunteers for a 'research project on attitudes towards food'. Half were sent a 'low fat diet' questionnaires (144 responded) and the other half were sent a 'five portions of fruit and vegetables' questionnaires (143 responded). Overall, about 70% of the sample were female, with ages ranging from 9 to 91 (mean age 41). Respondents were paid £5 on receipt of the completed questionnaires. Participants were sent two questionnaires, a month apart. The first questionnaire included demographic questions (age, gender and so on), questions designed to measure self-efficacy and locus of control, and questions about the extent to which the participants felt the need to eat less fat/eat five portions of fruit and vegetables per day. The second questionnaire was designed to measure the participants' actual diet and consisted of a 63-item food frequency survey. Povey *et al* mention the problems of using self-report measures in a study like this, but point out that a more objective way of measuring food intake would be very labour intensive and therefore expensive.

Results: For each of the two dietary

behaviours, locus of control and, especially, self-efficacy were good predictors of intentions. When it came to actual behaviour, high self-efficacy was significantly correlated with eating less fat and with eating more fruit and vegetables, but the correlation was weaker with behaviour than with intentions. Locus of control was not significantly correlated with actual behaviour.

Conclusions: Povey *et al* concluded that the Theory of Planned Behaviour can be applied to the two specific dietary behaviours they examined, and especially the self-efficacy component. They suggest that health promotion programmes aimed at improving diet should target people's sense of self-efficacy.

Real Life Application 2:

Anorexia nervosa

Anorexia nervosa is an eating disorder defined by the following symptoms:

- refusal to maintain body weight above 85% of the expected level
- intense fear of weight gain
- distorted body image (that is, thinking you are much fatter than you really are)
- amenorrhea (that is, no periods) for at least three months.

Roughly six people in 100,000 have anorexia, with ten times as many women as men suffering from the condition; eating disorders are also more common among higher social class groups. Jane Wardle suggests several different explanations for anorexia, and it is probably the case that a different combination of explanations applies to different people – that is, there is no single cause for the condition, or indeed most effective treatment, that applies to everyone. Some possible explanations for anorexia are listed below, under the headings used earlier in this section.

- **Genetics:** physiological abnormalities, such as

hormone imbalances, have been observed in people with anorexia. However, it is not clear whether these are causes of the eating disorder or effects of the low body weight and abnormal eating practices.

- **Behaviourist learning theory:** the fact the anorexia is so much more common in women may suggest that the causes are sociocultural rather than biological. For example, it is possible that an individual gains social reinforcement from being very thin (that is, approval, attention and so on) or else sees others gaining rewards for being thin (for example, fashion models). These two explanations, based respectively on the theories of operant conditioning and social learning, would be consistent with women suffering from anorexia more often than men.

- **Social influence:** although the proportion of women with anorexia is quite small, most women worry about their weight at some time. In the most 'at risk' age group (that is, young adult women), extreme dietary restriction, binge eating and even self-induced vomiting are not uncommon. Conformity may have a strong role to play for some women in their desire to be very thin.

- **Emotional factors:** feminist analyses of eating disorders have described them as understandable responses by women to the constraints of women's social roles and to the cultural ideals of female beauty. One suggestion by Susie Orbach (1978) is that anorexia is a way of rejecting the female sexual role, by refusing to develop a 'womanly' physique and to maintain normal menstruation. This theory suggests that anorexia may be a type of ego defence mechanism.

- **Cognitive theories:** without referring to the specific theories mentioned above, there are several ways in which a person's cognitions may contribute to an eating disorder. The most obvious one is people's perceptions of how fat they really are; there is evidence that anorexic women overestimate their own body size, but not other people's. It is also possible that anorexia is linked to the individual's sense of personal control. For example, women who have a very external locus of control or a low sense of self-efficacy are likely to feel disempowered and vulnerable in society; it may be that controlling their own appetite and contradicting the demands of their bodies gives them a greater sense of personal control (although

most people would argue that this sense of control is illusory).

Adapted from 'Anorexia nervosa and bulimia' by Jane Wardle, 1997.

Summary

- Anorexia is a serious condition that is much more common in women than in men.
- Psychologists have come up with a wide range of explanations for the condition, varying from purely biological, to cognitive and social.
- For an individual with anorexia, the causes probably consist of an interaction between several different types of factor.
- Effective treatment for anorexia needs to address both the eating behaviour and the underlying attitudes, and will vary from person to person.

Questions

1 How can you tell if someone has got anorexia nervosa?

2 Suggest appropriate treatments for anorexia, linked to each of the possible explanations described in RLA 2.

Cultural factors affecting health

The previous section focused on ways in which behaviours and lifestyles may affect health. Related to this are the cultural factors that might influence these ways of living. In particular this section will focus on gender, ethnicity, class and age, and how these factors influence inequalities in health and health care.

There have been a number of recent reports looking at health issues in Great Britain, many of them initiated by the government. For example *The Health of the Nation*, published in 1992, is the government's strategy for health in England and Wales. Some of its targets have to take account of differences in mortality rates among different groups in the population – social class is very important in this respect. *Inequalities in Health*, published in 1999, is a series of papers that makes up the evidence presented to the Independent Inquiry into Inequalities in Health, chaired by Sir Donald Acheson. This inquiry makes a number of recommendations based on its findings, most of which address the need to reduce poverty among certain sections of the population.

It is, of course, important to recognize that gender, ethnicity, social class and age all intersect to some degree. However, in terms of health and health-related behaviours, being a young working class white woman is quite different from being an elderly middle class Asian male.

Gender and health

Gender is a cultural factor. Although sex is obviously a **biological** category, the illnesses that women suffer can sometimes be related to their **role** in society, which is a cultural construct. The health of women is quite different to the health of men in many ways, and this affects their use of the health services; therefore, it is also important to look at the provision of health care for women. Women and men differ in their illness and mortality rates, and many of these differences reflect social and cultural differences between women and men – for example:

- women outlive men in our society by about five to six years
- men between the ages of fifteen and forty-four have a three to four times higher mortality rate than women from accidents, suicide and violence (Arber, 1999)
- women suffer from more reported mental health problems than men – they are more likely to be referred to a psychiatrist or therapist than men, and are more likely to be prescribed psychotropic drugs (Ussher, 1997)
- men report higher levels of alcohol and drug dependence.

Biological differences

There are, of course, **biological differences** that affect the illnesses, needs and the provision of health services for men and women. For example, health care for women has largely focused on their reproductive needs, and all the associated services, such as contraception, abortion and infertility. 'Well women' clinics provide screening services that are focused on women's biological differences from men – cervical and breast screening. Many researchers would argue that this reproductive focus has meant that women's health in other areas has been neglected. Illnesses that have historically been associated with men, such as coronary heart disease, have had more attention. Interestingly, there has been relatively little attention focused on men's

reproductive needs, and there are very few 'well men' clinics, for example.

Cultural/psychosocial differences

More important perhaps are the **social** and **environmental influences** on health that have little to do with biological differences. Gender roles and relationships affect both women's and men's health. There are a number of ways in which women's roles affect their health, such as the fact that women are stereotyped by society as 'carers'. Because of this they often find themselves caring for sick or elderly relatives and they are, by and large, the unpaid carers of young children. Women are more often on the receiving end of domestic violence than men, and many women bring up young children alone. All these examples inevitably mean that women are placed in a position where their health and the health of those that they care for may suffer.

There are particular physical and mental health problems for carers, such as exhaustion and stress. Lone parents, particularly women, can suffer from low **self-esteem** and lack of **social support** when they are outside the job market and they may lack the economic resources to take part in many activities most people take for granted. Male carers may also suffer unique disadvantages – for example, men often have different types of friendship to women and these may be less easy to rely on at times of ill health (Arber, 1999).

Biological or psychosocial explanation?

Some conditions that women suffer from have been examined from both a **biological** and a **psychosocial** perspective, and these make an interesting comparison – in particular conditions such as premenstrual syndrome (PMS), postnatal depression (PND) and the menopause. With all of these conditions **medical** interpretations focus on the biochemical changes associated with hormonal levels. According to the medical model, these hormonal changes account for the psychological and physical problems reported by women. However, it can be argued from a psychosocial approach that there are more complex relationships between a range of factors that may affect physical and psychological symptoms.

Ussher (1997) has carried out an interesting review of the literature in relation to the three conditions listed above. She argues that in relation to pre-menstrual syndrome, it can be disputed that there is a simple causal relationship between hormonal changes and PMS. In treatment trials for PMS there are studies that show that placebo treatments were as effective, if not more effective, than active treatments. From a psychosocial perspective in relation to pre-menstrual syndrome, Ussher argues that attribution (that is, locus of control – see page 15) can also explain symptoms, with the attribution of negative feelings to the menstrual cycle and positive ones to external circumstances.

With postnatal depression there is a similar problem with a biological explanation that relies on an imbalance in hormones. Many of the symptoms of postnatal depression can also be attributed to the social and psychological upheavals of a new baby and the responsibilities of childcare.

A number of studies have shown that during the menopause relatively few physical symptoms (hot flushes and vaginal dryness) are related to hormonal changes. From a psychosocial perspective, studies show that psychological symptoms such as depression and anxiety are no more severe during the menopause than at any other time.

One of the important factors to consider in this review is the fact that not all women suffer equally from these symptoms, and according to Ussher, this shows very clearly the importance of psychosocial explanations. Key Study 2 illustrates this clearly.

KEY STUDY 2

Researcher: Ruble (1977)

Aim: To examine the physiological basis of pre-menstrual symptoms, and to question the validity of women's self-reports of these symptoms.

Method: Some 44 women undergraduates at Princeton University aged 18 to 24 were told they were taking part in research looking at a technique for predicting the expected date of menstruation. The research was carried out in the university infirmary. The women were interviewed (unknown to them) on the sixth or seventh day before their next period (calculated on the basis of previous information given to the researchers). The participants were randomly assigned to different experimental groups – pre-menstrual (one to two days until next period), intermenstrual (seven to ten days until next period) or control (given no information). They were 'tested' using an EEG machine, and told to which group they belonged. The women were then given a questionnaire in which they had to rate the extent to which they had experienced the symptoms in the questionnaire. It was predicted that the women who were told they were pre-menstrual would report experiencing higher levels of certain symptoms compared to the intermenstrual women.

Results: The results confirmed the predictions. Symptom rating of women who thought they were pre-menstrual was significantly higher than those who had been told they were intermenstrual for the symptoms of water retention, pain and change in eating habits.

Conclusions: Although Ruble recognized that demand characteristics may have affected the results of her study, she argued that the results show that learned associations or beliefs can cause a woman to overstate what she is actually experiencing or affect a woman's actual perception of her own body when she believes she is pre-menstrual. Ruble argues that this demonstrates that the extent to which psychological or physiological factors influence the pre-menstrual phase is open to question.

Health care provision for men and women

As has been noted earlier (see page 19), the provision of health care for women has traditionally focused on their reproductive role. A further point that is interesting in the context of gender differences is that men and women suffering from the same condition may receive quite different treatment. Arber (1999) notes that women in the US are less likely to receive kidney transplants than men, and that in the UK women are less likely than men to be offered a coronary artery bypass if they have heart disease. She also reports that women have appeared in very little research on AIDS or coronary heart disease. Many areas of research appear gender blind.

One area of concern is the need for appropriate medical care for elderly women. Although women live longer than men, they tend to become more disabled in older age than men. Chronic illness restricts independence, and older women suffer more restrictive and debilitating conditions than men. Statistics from 1994 show that 15% of women over 65 compared to 8.5% of men over 65 suffered disability that needed daily help (Arber, 1999). Older men are also more likely to have the financial resources to pay for this help or to have a wife who can provide it (more older women are widowed).

All of these examples show that in spite of the fact that most health care policies are assumed to be gender free, it is obvious that there is considerable bias in the provision of health care resources. Moreover, to a considerable degree stereotyping and societal expectations lie at the root of this.

Commentary

- **Stereotyping** of men and women in terms of the norms and expectations of society is particularly problematic, since it can lead to misdiagnosis and labelling of illnesses. For example, women are more likely to be given a psychological diagnosis for a non-specific problem, whereas a man will be given a medical one. Labels can mean that the real cause of the problem is ignored.

- Biological explanations of gender differences are reductionist. It is too simple to assume that hormones are the cause of a specific condition. There appear to be much more multidimensional causes for particular illnesses. This is not to deny the importance of biological factors, but rather to acknowledge that other explanations may be as important to consider.

Ethnicity and health

Many studies suggest that there is a strong link between ethnicity and health. Within and between cultures there are many different practices that affect health and well-being. As early as 1982 the World Health Organization recognized the importance of understanding cultural differences in terms of successful health policies and interventions:

If actions are to be effective in the prevention of disease and the promotion of health and well-being, they must be based on an understanding of culture, tradition, beliefs and patterns of family interaction (1982, p. 4).

There is some debate as to how much difference there is in rates of ill health and mortality between ethnic minority groups within the UK. Bennett and Murphy (1997) suggest there is considerable difference, while Nazroo (1999) argues that the difference between groups is exaggerated. Bennett and Murphy suggest that coronary heart disease among Indians is 36% higher for men and 46% higher for women than the national average. For Afro-Caribbeans, they suggest that the incidence of strokes is 76% higher for men and 110% higher for women than the national average. Nazroo, however, suggests that the similarities between minority and majority groups outweigh the differences, and that to highlight these contrasts suggests different causes and solutions, which can marginalize and stigmatize certain groups.

Biological differences

Some disorders show that there is a genetic link between the incidence of these illnesses and ethnicity. For example, people of Afro-Caribbean descent have higher rates of sickle cell anaemia and Asians have higher rates of thalassaemia than the general population. Another example is the incidence of a disorder called Tay-Sachs disease in the Jewish population. This is a rare genetic disorder in which the sufferer cannot produce a crucial enzyme, which means that their life expectancy is only three or four years. About 1 in 250 people in the general population carries one copy of the Tay-Sachs gene; in the Jewish population this is about 1 in 25. Carriers are healthy, but if a child inherits two copies of the gene it will develop this condition (Senior and Vivash, 1998).

Commentary

There are conditions that also appear to be more prevalent in certain ethnic groups than others, but where there is a less clear genetic link than for sickle cell anaemia, thalassaemia and Tay-Sachs. These are illustrated by the cases of coronary heart disease and strokes cited earlier. However, it must be recognized that although some people might be genetically vulnerable to some of these conditions, whether they develop them or not depends on a number of other factors such as environment, and health behaviours such as diet.

Cultural/psychosocial differences

Although some of the genetic bio-medical explanations place too much emphasis on difference in their approach to understanding the health of people from ethnic minority backgrounds, it is none the less important to be sensitive to the particular needs of different ethnic minority groups in terms of particular health care issues. For example, there may be communication problems with a general practitioner, or cultural differences in the expression of symptoms – making diagnostic techniques used in a Western medical approach inappropriate.

Nazroo points out that ethnic groups are not all or equally at risk of ill health or mortality. Data suggests that as a group, Indians have good health overall, and for some illnesses certain ethnic minorities are better off than the general population. For example, few Asian women smoke, and therefore they have low rates of respiratory illnesses compared to the majority. One problem, however, is that the data for ethnic minority populations is relatively recent, and so long-term trends have yet to emerge. This is because most immigration to the UK happened in the 1950s.

One problem that affects many people from minority backgrounds is racism. Brown (1994) argues that racism in the form of racial harassment and discrimination may have an effect on health in the form of stress or personal injury. This is very hard to quantify, but there is evidence to suggest that this cannot be overlooked.

Nazroo looks at the geographical location of people from ethnic minorities, and argues that the concentration of ethnic minority groups in particular areas might offer some protection from the stressful effects of racism, through social support and a strong sense of community. Relative household size and composition may also be beneficial in this respect.

Additionally, it is important to look at social class as an explanation of health differences in terms of ethnicity. This is because a significant proportion of people from ethnic minority backgrounds are in social classes IV and V (semi-skilled and un-skilled manual workers). Therefore problems that affect these classes affect people from these groups also.

Access to health care

There is some evidence to suggest that there is inequality in access to health care for ethnic minority groups compared to the majority of the population. A number of studies suggest that ethnic minority people are less likely to be referred on by their GP, less likely to receive a follow-up appointment,

One of the recommendations made to the Acheson Inquiry was that more ethnic minority workers should be recruited into the health service.

and spend less time with their GP than white people. Some of this might be related to the communication problems mentioned above, but it may be the case that this is an illustration of indirect racism.

Commentary

- It is important to recognize the multifactoral explanation for health inequalities in terms of ethnicity. Biological explanations can only be understood in conjunction with cultural differences. Culture changes and health behaviours will be influenced by many things, both part of the minority and the majority cultures. Health behaviours are also influenced by gender and social class, and socioeconomic factors must not be underestimated.
- Some of the recommendations made to the Acheson Inquiry (1998) suggest that health professionals should receive more training in order to discover what is relevant to a particular culture, that ethnic minority doctors should be supported as much as possible, and that more ethnic minority workers should be recruited into the health service.

Social class and health

There is a great deal of contemporary evidence to suggest that health varies according to socioeconomic status. It could be argued that it is the single most important factor that explains health and illness. To be homeless and to live 'rough' carries a higher risk of mortality than any other group in the population. Any index of socioeconomic status (including home and car ownership, income or class classification) appears to show similar trends – that is, the better the material circumstances, the lower the rate of premature mortality.

The Department of Health's report *Variations in Health* (1995) shows that of 66 major causes of death among men, 62 were most common among men in social class IV and V. Of 70 major causes of death among women, 64 were most common among women married to men in class IV and V (cited in Senior and Vivash, 1998). As is described in more detail later (see page 24), children are similarly disadvantaged by their social class position. Deaths caused by respiratory diseases and accidents are the most highly correlated with social class. The lower the social class the higher the risk.

Although the number of people in class V is reducing, the health gap between social class I and social class V is widening (Trowler, 1996). The only exception to this general trend is that the class differences in the deaths of babies under one year of age has narrowed considerably in recent years.

Explanations for inequality

The most obvious cause of class inequalities in health is the differential access to resources between the different social classes. People in classes IV and V often have too little household income, live in unsafe, cold and damp housing, work in jobs where they are more likely to have accidents than people in other social classes, smoke and drink more as a result of stress, and are more likely to suffer from a major 'life event' (see page 81) that will then affect their health.

A further explanation is that the areas in which poorer people live are often those that have inadequate health services. The health service has its own hierarchy, and the best research and training hospitals are not always located where they are most needed.

There is also research to suggest that people in different social classes are treated differently by health professionals. Middle class people tend to be more demanding of the health service in terms of information and doctors' surgery time, for example. Doctors have been shown to respond to the questions of middle class people by answering questions and discussing treatments more fully.

One of the most convincing, but also one of the most problematic, explanations is that people in different social classes behave in ways that lead to worse health than people in other social classes. People in classes IV and V, for example, are more

likely to behave in ways that damage their health (as has already been described) by smoking and drinking to excess, and eating a poor diet.

Commentary

One of the problems with any explanation that focuses on the behaviour of a group of people is that it is likely to place 'blame' on that group for their particular health behaviours. However, there are considerable behavioural differences within, as well as between, social classes. The behaviour of poorer members of society is limited by factors that are often beyond their control, such as the availability of transport and shops.

Psychosocial explanations of inequality

It is not only material factors that explain the behaviours and health of people in classes IV and V. There are a number of other factors that are also important to consider. One of these is how people feel about their 'relative' position in society. Research tends to suggest that it is not only absolute deprivation that matters. Evidence from Japan and other similarly affluent countries suggests that longest life expectancy occurs in places with the most equitable income distribution. As Wilkinson states:

It looks as if what matters about our physical circumstances is not what they are in themselves, but where they stand in the scale of things in our society. The implication is that our environment and standard of living no longer impact on our health primarily through direct physical causes, regardless of our attitudes and perceptions, but have come to do so mainly through social and cognitively mediated processes (1990, p. 405, cited in Carroll et al, 1993).

Wilkinson appears to be suggesting that it is the individuals' response to their relative positions that is important. For example, the stress caused by an awareness of socioeconomic position and the way in which it limits opportunities may threaten health. Feelings of low self-esteem and lack of personal control may also be important. Unemployment, therefore, should not only be considered in terms of material deprivation, but also in terms of the sense of powerlessness that is created for individuals who lose their jobs.

Age and health

It is important to look at the different ways in which age can affect health, and to consider the nature of health at particular stages of life. Although it can be argued that age is a 'social construct' in as much as age is classified into what may be considered to be fairly arbitrary categories – for example, infants, children, adults and the elderly – these categories do appear to have particular patterns of ill health and mortality. It is important to understand these trends and differences because of the implications for the health service, for example. A growing proportion of the population in many countries is elderly, and the needs of this ageing population must therefore be understood. It is worth noting here that any analysis of age-related health issues also appears to take account of social class.

Childhood

Children (along with the elderly) use the health service more than other age groups in the population. Some of this is to receive preventive care – such as vaccinations – but children are also more likely to be taken to the doctor by a worried parent who is unsure about symptoms than an adult is to visit the doctor. Social class is an important consideration here, as there is a great deal of evidence to suggest that children in social classes IV and V are more disadvantaged in their health than children in classes I and II. For example:

- mortality rates for infants and children differ by social class, with mortality rates being higher in social classes IV and V
- children of parents in social class IV and V suffer more chronic illness than children from social classes I and II (ONS, 1997)
- mothers of children in manual classes are more likely to smoke during pregnancy (associated with low birth weight and a higher incidence of Sudden Infant Death Syndrome)
- children of parents in social classes IV and V are more likely to suffer both fatal and non-fatal accidents than children of parents in social classes I and II.

Law argues that 'The majority of [parents] … living in poverty wish to, and do, protect and promote the health of their children under the most unpromising conditions' (1999, p. 5). However, she suggests that one way to help parents in this situation is to offer personal support. She reviews the literature, some of which suggests that women who receive social support from a trained person during pregnancy have shorter labours and that their babies had a higher APGAR score post-delivery (that is, were rated as

more robust by midwives just after birth). Some studies have tried to use social support to reduce stress and raise self-esteem in new mothers. Women receiving social support were found to be happier and more likely to be breast-feeding after birth than a control group (Elbourne *et al* 1989, cited in Law, 1999).

Adulthood

In adulthood, social class continues to be important, although perhaps less so in adolescence and young adulthood. In adolescence, there are some indications that social class matters – for example, in relation to mortality rates. For boys aged between 10 and 15 these are 15 per 1,000,000 in social class I compared to 41 per 100,000 in social class V (Drever and Whitehead, 1997). However, there are many ways in which social class does not appear to be a factor – in relation to non-fatal accidents and emotional disorders, for example.

Some health behaviours that are associated with adolescence are not clearly related to social class – for example, smoking, drinking and drug use. A study of 12–15 and 16–19 year olds in Glasgow found that 'experience of drugs' was highest in the second most affluent and the poorest area of the city (Carey personal communication, cited in West, 1999). Other health behaviours, however, do appear to be more closely related to social class – for example, diet, exercise and sexual behaviour. Adolescents from classes IV and V are more likely to have intercourse at a younger age than adolescents from social classes I and II (Johnson *et al*, 1994).

As adults, the differences begin to emerge more strongly. One of the interesting features of adult illness and mortality is that the behaviour that influences this is related to present class position, but the physiological predisposition may be genetic or relate to childhood class position (Blane, 1999). However, current class position seems to be the strongest indicator. For example, 'early' mortality rates are much higher in social class V than in social class I. Blane argues that factors such as stress increasingly account for illness and disease in our society. He argues that this often relates to the workplace, as there is less job security than there used to be. Working in employment that is not secure can be very stressful, as is unemployment. This is backed up by other research findings that suggest that unemployment is closely related to poorer mental health (West, 1999).

Old age

Elderly people have specific problems as a group, not only because their health varies according to social class (although this is more difficult to measure in people past retirement age), but also because as a group they have less access to resources within the health service than younger people.

Research shows that social class inequalities remain in old age. For example, life expectancy differs by 2 to 3 years, after the age of 65, between social class I and V (Khaw, 1999). There are many socioeconomic factors that can indicate social position in old age. A study by Fletcher *et al* (1997) showed that men and women in rented accommodation, and without access to a car, had a 50% higher mortality rate than people who owned their own home and car.

Health-related behaviours such as diet are linked to income, and studies that look at the diets of elderly people suggest that many pensioners have diets that are similar to the lowest income groups. For example, they have a high consumption of fats, meat, sugar and cereals. Smoking is also related to class – 16% of men and 14% of women in social class I smoke, compared to 40% of men and 34% of women in social class V (Khaw, 1999).

Access to health services is also a problem for all elderly people. For example, 90% of elderly patients who need treatment for incontinence do not receive it (McGrother *et al*, 1994), and eye problems such as glaucoma and cataracts often go undiagnosed. Social class is also a factor in relation to access – for example, women in class I have a much better ten-year survival rate for breast cancer, compared to five-year survival rate for women in class V (Schrijvers *et al*, 1995).

Policies to alleviate some of these problems recommend the need for lifestyle changes such as better nutrition, and environmental changes such as better housing in old age (Khaw, 1999).

Commentary

Social class, and its inevitable relationship with deprivation and poverty, appears to be the factor that accounts for the differences in the health status of all age groups. There is an obvious problem with the categorization of age groups as this is very culturally specific, and it is therefore difficult to generalize the findings from studies on age to other societies. A good example of this is the way in which old people are marginalized in Britain, and have the highest status in some other societies. There is also a problem with stereotyping age groups and making assumptions about their needs. Health care policies are often designed to meet the needs of the stereotypical 'young' person – sex or drugs education, for example. The wishes of 'old' people are often ignored, as health care professionals and others assume they know what is best.

Essay questions

1 Using specific examples, discuss genetic and environmental influences on health-related behaviour.

2 Describe and evaluate ways in which cognitive factors can influence health related behaviour.

3 Choosing two of the four factors, discuss the ways in which gender, ethnicity, age and class might affect health.

Promoting health

This chapter examines models of health promotion, including the way in which health messages can be communicated effectively to their target audience, using examples of workplace and school campaigns. It also applies psychological theories to an understanding of exercise and nutrition. Additionally, the chapter examines why people misuse substances, and ways of preventing and treating substance misuse. Finally, the chapter looks at psychological issues relating to health and safety, such as personality and accident proneness. Real Life Applications that are considered are:

- RLA 3: Sun know how
- RLA 4: Workplace smoking bans
- RLA 5: A gene for alcoholism?
- RLA 6: The use of cycle helmets

Health promotion

The section entitled 'Improving health' in Chapter 1 (see pages 5–6) described three ways in which people's health can be promoted – that is, advances in medical science, behavioural changes and social change. Naidoo and Wills (2000) describe five different models of health promotion:

- the medical model
- the behaviour change model
- the educational model
- the empowerment model
- the social change model.

The first of these models aims to improve health through advancements in medical science; the next three all aim at getting individuals to lead healthier lives, but take slightly different approaches in order to achieve this aim; and the fifth model argues that health improvements should occur through social and economic change.

The empowerment and social change models reflect a **radical** approach to health promotion, in that they are based in the belief that ill health arises out of power inequalities in society, and that health promotion should be concerned with changing society, either as a result of grass roots initiatives or organized political change. The behaviour change and educational models reflect a **social regulation** approach to health promotion in that they focus on modifying individual behaviour and cognitions, and

make use of psychological theory. The political arguments relating to these two types of approaches are beyond the scope of this book. The fact that the rest of this book is based on the social regulation approach, focusing on changing individual behaviour rather than inequalities in society, does not imply an acceptance of its underlying political assumptions, but a recognition that this is a book about health psychology and not about politics.

Models of health promotion

1 **The medical model:** this approach aims to reduce illness and premature death and operates at three levels. **Primary prevention** attempts to stop people from getting ill in the first place (for example, by immunization or by taking vitamins); **secondary prevention** attempts to catch the disease early enough so that it can be treated (for example, cancer screening); **tertiary prevention** attempts to minimize the debilitating effects once an illness has taken hold (for example, palliative care or rehabilitation). This approach is based on the medical model of health (see Chapter 1, page 1), and although it has been responsible for a very significant improvement in people's health, it suffers from the same limitations as the medical model (for example, it focuses on preventing disease rather than promoting positive health, and it ignores psychological and environmental factors).

2 **The behaviour change model**: like the medical model, this approach is 'top down', in that health 'experts' decide which behaviours are good or bad for health, then try to get people to change their lifestyles accordingly. A problem with this kind of prescriptive approach is that it undermines individuals' autonomy and it assumes that the experts always know best.

3 **The educational model**: this is also aimed at changing people's lifestyles but, unlike the behaviour change model which is **instructional** (that is, deciding what is good for people, then telling them to do it), it provides individuals with knowledge, information and skills so that they can make their own informed decisions about how to behave. This model assumes that individuals are able to make free choices once they are in full possession of the facts, but this ignores emotional, environmental, social and economic constraints. Also, in principle it must allow individuals to make an informed choice to lead an unhealthy lifestyle if they wish to, but in practice health educators tend to have a particular lifestyle in mind when they are presenting people with information (for example, a health education teacher who tells a group of children about the dangers of smoking would feel that he or she has failed if some of the children make an 'informed choice' to carry on smoking).

4 **The empowerment model**: this is a third approach aimed at getting people to lead healthier lives but, unlike the other two, it is a 'bottom-up', non-directive, client-centred approach. The role of the empowering health educator is to help people realize that they themselves would like to change their situation, and to help them develop the skills and confidence to do so. It helps individuals gain more control over their own lives in the hope that they will be naturally drawn towards a healthier existence.

5 **The social change model**: this radical approach recognizes the strong links between health and the social and economic environment, and attempts to improve the former by dealing with the latter.

Communicating health messages

The previous section describes different models of health promotion; currently, it is the **behaviour change** model and the **educational** model that are most often used, and central to both these models is the issue of **communication**: both models depend on imparting information to people in order to bring about behavioural change. The key role of communication in health promotion also applies to other areas of human activity, such as **advertising** and **political propaganda** (for an interesting discussion of both these issues see Banyard, 1999), and this has led to a great deal of research over the years about how to communicate with maximum effectiveness. For example, James Hartley has written many books and papers on how to design text, covering such issues as what typeface to use, how to lay out text, diagrams and pictures, how to write as clearly and simply as possible and so on (for example see Hartley, 1994). However, theories about the psychology of communication are still largely based on work carried out in the 1950s at Yale University, USA.

The Yale Communication Research Program was set up in the early 1950s as a response to the increasing role of mass communication in economic, political and social spheres. Advertising was developing into big business, and the Cold War meant that Americans were becoming increasingly paranoid about the need to counteract 'foreign propaganda'. Also, agencies such as UNESCO (United Nations Educational, Scientific and Cultural Organization) were developing mass educational programmes, and there was a growing recognition of the need to counteract racial and religious prejudice in the US. The key findings of the Yale Communication Research Program are set out in a book called *Communication and persuasion* (Hovland, Janis and Kelley, 1953) and are described below.

The Yale Model of Communication

Hovland *et al* (1953) focus on three aspects of communication – the communicator (who says it); the communication (what is said); the audience (to whom is it said):

- **The communicator:** the crucial factor here seems to be the **credibility** of the source of the information. Low credibility sources are seen as more biased and unfair, and have a much weaker effect on the audience's opinions than high credibility sources; in research studies audiences learnt as much information from high and low credibility communicators, but were much more likely to accept the conclusions advocated if the credibility of the source was high (although, these difference tended to disappear after a few weeks). This means that health messages that come from a credible source are more likely to be believed, at least in the short term.

There are several ways of convincing an audience that a source of communication is credible – quoting academic or professional qualifications (for example, using a doctor to explain why it is important to eat a healthy diet), using people who have had relevant personal experience (for example, using ex-drug addicts to talk to young people about substance use), or using people who are generally perceived as trustworthy and honest (this means that if celebrities are used in health promotion programmes, their public image needs to be carefully considered).

- **The communication:** the Health Belief Model (see Chapter 1, pages 11–13) says that perceived threat (made up of perceived seriousness and perceived susceptibility) is a prerequisite for healthy behaviour – in other words, people will not change their lifestyles unless they believe that they will become unhealthy unless they do so. The Theory of Planned Behaviour also includes perceived threat as a key factor. The most obvious way to persuade someone that their health is at risk is through **fear arousal**, and it seems reasonable to conclude that the content of health promotion communications should include fear arousal.

The role of fear arousal is not just to trigger the individual to make a cognitive decision to change his or her behaviour, but to arouse **emotional tension**, the theory being that the individual will change his or her behaviour in order to reduce this tension. Indeed, it is commonly believed that the more you frighten people, the more likely they are to change their behaviour; almost all health promotion campaigns contain an element of fear arousal, and some are very frightening indeed.

However, research has been done that suggests that strong fear arousal can be counter-productive (see Key Study 3). If a fear arousing message is so frightening that it creates a degree of emotional tension that the individual cannot deal with through behaviour change, then he or she uses ego defence mechanisms (see Chapter 1, pages 10–11) to cope; this avoidance actually reduces the chance of behavioural change. For example, if teenagers are shown an anti-smoking video containing graphic images of people dying from smoking-related diseases, but this does not very effectively tell them how to give up smoking

KEY STUDY 3

Researchers: Janis and Feshbach (1953)

Aim: To study the motivational effect of fear arousal in health promotion communications in order to determine whether the emotional tension caused by fear arousal leads to a change in behaviour (to decrease tension), or whether people tend to use avoidance techniques instead.

Method: The entire 'freshman' class of a large Connecticut high school was randomly divided into four groups (mean age approximately 15, roughly equal numbers of males and females). Three of the groups were given a 15-minute illustrated lecture on tooth decay, and the importance of oral hygiene. The fourth group acted as a control. The three experimental groups were given different forms of the lecture:

* Form 1 – strong fear appeal, emphasizing the painful consequences of tooth decay and gum disease
* Form 2 – moderate fear appeal, in which the dangers were described in a milder and more factual manner
* Form 3 – minimal fear appeal, which rarely alluded to the consequences of tooth neglect. Participants were given a questionnaire one week before the lecture (asking them about dental hygiene) a second questionnaire immediately after the lecture (asking about the immediate effects of the communication), and a third questionnaire one week after the lecture (asking whether their oral hygiene behaviour had changed).

Results: Janis and Feshbach found that higher levels of fear arousal resulted in greater anxiety about tooth decay immediately after the lecture (an increase of 42% of the 'strong fear' group who felt 'somewhat or very worried' compared to an increase of 24% for the 'minimal fear' group). There were no differences in the amount of information each group acquired from the lecture, but the 'strong fear' group appraised the communication more favourably than the other groups on a number of questions (for example, 'interesting', 'did a good job' and so on), but also thought that the lecture was more 'horrible' and 'disgusting'. However, when it came to assessing behaviour change, the 'minimal fear' communication was most effective: change in conformity to oral hygiene behaviour was 36% for the 'minimal fear', 22% for the 'moderate fear', 8% for the 'strong fear' and 0% for the control group.

Conclusions: The overall effectiveness of a health promotion communication is likely to be reduced by the use of a strong fear appeal. Janis and Feshbach argue that this is because when fear is strongly aroused but is not fully relieved by reassurances contained in the communication, the audience will become motivated to ignore or to minimize the importance of the threat.

themselves, the only way they can deal with the stress is through avoidance. They might use a process of **rationalization** (for example, 'It's only old people on the video – it won't happen to me') or **suppression** (for example, by messing around and not paying attention to the video).

Apart from fear arousal, Hovland *et al* (1953) mention other important features of the content of communication. For example, they investigated whether it is more effective to state a specific conclusion explicitly or whether it is better to leave it to be drawn by the audience. They found that in communications that deal with complicated issues, it is better for the communicator to spell out the conclusions rather than rely on the audience, and this is particularly true when the audience is less well-informed or less 'intelligent'. On the other hand, when the message is fairly simple, or when addressing well-informed people, it is more effective to let the audience reach its own conclusions. This means that, in deciding how directive to be in a health promotion message, it is important to consider the complexity of the message and the nature of the audience.

Another factor is the extent to which the audience actively participates in the communication; the more participation there is, then the more the messages are **internalized**. This means that it is better to involve the audience in some way, maybe through discussion, or even asking them to repeat the message to others. Most health promotion messages are communicated through media that are really 'one-way', such as leaflets, posters and videos. However, even with such material it is possible to get some audience participation, or at least the perception of it. For example, many health promotions leaflets use the technique of posing questions as if they have come from the person reading the leaflet, and then answering them. As long as these questions seem relevant to the individual, and are the kinds of question they would ask if they could, then s/he will have the illusion that s/he is actively participating in the communication process, and may take more note of the messages being given. Another technique sometimes used in health promotion leaflets is to ask the reader to answer personal questions by ticking boxes on the leaflet.

• **The audience:** Hovland *et al* (1953) found that certain individuals are more susceptible to persuasion than others. For example, people with low self-esteem, depressive tendencies and 'social inadequacies' are more likely to be influenced by persuasive communications. Also, people with a strong sense of group conformity will be more resistant to messages that are contrary to the standards and beliefs of the group.

These findings have interesting implications for health promotion: if people with low self-esteem, for example, are more likely to respond to health promotion messages, why is it that such people tend to lead less healthy lifestyles? Apart from the fact that self-esteem may be related to health behaviour for all sorts of complex reasons, it must be remembered that the amount of time and money spent on health promotion in our society is a tiny fraction of that spent on commercial advertising. Furthermore, people are constantly bombarded with messages from other media sources. We receive many more messages promoting unhealthy lifestyles than healthy ones, and so it makes sense that individuals who are more susceptible to persuasive communication lead less healthy lives; rather than attempt to 'counter-persuade' such people, it may be better to help them regain their self-esteem, so that they become more resistant to negative health messages.

In conclusion, the Yale Model of Communication holds the following specific implications for designing health promotion campaigns:

- It is important that the source of the information is perceived as credible by the audience.
- A low level of fear arousal is necessary in order to trigger perceived threat, but too much fear will cause high levels of tension, leading to avoidance.
- If a message is complex, or the audience not very well-informed, then conclusions need to be explicitly stated. Otherwise, it is better to let the audience reach its own conclusions.
- Certain individuals (for example, with low self-esteem) are easier to persuade than others, but they are as likely to be influenced by negative health messages (from advertising and the media) as by health promotion messages.
- If possible, it is best to involve the audience in active participation in the communicationprocess.

RLA 3 shows how some of these communication principles can be put into practice.

Commentary

It is possible to question the morality of advertising or propaganda on the grounds that they are attempting to manipulate people's consumer behaviour or political and social activity. Can the use of persuasive communication in health promotion be criticized for the same reasons? Unlike advertising and propaganda, which are carried out in the name of profit or political influence, at least health promotion is specifically aimed at improving people's lives. However, there is a narrow line between legitimate research into ways of communicating more effectively, and using psychology to help manipulate people's behaviour and attitudes.

Exercise and nutrition

The human body has evolved over the years to become adapted to a certain lifestyle in terms of physical activity and diet. It is only very recently that mechanized transport and various labour-saving devices have been developed. For more than 90% of the 2 million years since humans have existed on earth, we lived a nomadic existence, hunting and gathering food. This means that most people's lifestyle in terms of diet and exercise is fundamentally different from that for which our bodies have evolved. There are still a few nomadic groups of people in existence, and they seem to be leaner, fitter and relatively free of the chronic diseases that are common in technologically developed societies. There is a widespread recognition in our society that our lives are too sedentary, and that we can improve our health by taking exercise and eating a certain diet, and many health promotion programmes are aimed at persuading people to change their behaviour in these respects.

Exercise

There are several different types of exercise, as listed below:

- **Aerobic:** this is exercise that stimulates the cardiovascular system (that is, the heart and lungs), such as running, cycling, swimming and some active sports. A leaflet produced by the Department of Health (1998) aimed at men over 40 suggests at least 30 minutes of moderate aerobic activity (for example, climbing stairs, walking the dog, gardening) five days a week.
- **Anaerobic:** this is physical activity that does not require high levels of oxygen because there is little body movement – for example, yoga.
- **Isotonic:** this builds up strength and endurance by moving a heavy object in one direction – for example, weight lifting, press-ups.
- **Isometric:** this is designed to build up strength rather than endurance, and involves exerting a force against an immovable object.
- **Isokinetic:** this involves using muscular force to move an object in more than one direction for example, pushing a bar backwards and forwards.

Physiological benefits of exercise

Paffenbarger et al (1986) (cited in Ogden, 1996, p. 141) found in a longitudinal study that people who took regular exercise lived an average of 2.5 years longer than people who led very sedentary lives.

Real Life Application 3: Sun know how

sun know how

FACT CARD

- Skin cancer is the second most common cancer in the UK
- The number of new cases increases every year and has doubled in the past 20 years
- The cause of skin cancer is nearly always over exposure to ultraviolet radiation – from the sun or a sunbed
- Ultraviolet radiation is reflected off light coloured surfaces, especially water, sand and snow – this increases it's strength
- You can still get sunburnt through light cloud or under shallow water – protect yourself when swimming
- There is nothing healthy about a suntan. Your skin darkens because it has been damaged
- Most cases of skin cancer could be easily prevented

PROTECT YOURSELF AND FOLLOW THE SUN SAFETY CODE

COVER UP – with loose, cool clothing to keep the sun off your skin. Wear a hat, preferably with a wide brim and sunglasses (BS2724:1987)

PROTECT CHILDREN – they are particularly vulnerable. Sunburn during childhood can lead to skin cancer later in life. Keep babies out of the sun completely.

SEEK SHADE – especially during the hottest part of the day, from 11am to 3pm.

USE A SUNSCREEN – SPF 15 or higher on any exposed skin. Use it an hour before going outside and reapply it frequently and generously.

TAKE CARE NOT TO BURN – sunburn increases your risk of skin cancer

BE AWARE OF YOUR SKIN. If you have a mole that is changing size, shape, colour, itching or bleeding – see your doctor. If skin cancers are treated early, they should cause you no further problems.

TAKE SPECIAL CARE:

- Of children and babies, they spend longer outdoors and burn easily
- If you have very pale skin, fair or red hair
- If you have a lot of moles or freckles
- If you have had skin cancer before, or you have a family history of it
- If you work or spend a lot of time outdoors

FACT: Brown or black skinned people rarely get skin cancer, however they should still take care in the hot sun.

FACT: The sun also causes thickening of the skin leading to premature ageing and wrinkles.

FACT: Too much sun can also cause heat exhaustion, skin irritation and sun stroke – especially in the very young.

Enjoy the sun but take it easy – skin cancer kills approximately 2000 people every year in the UK.

sun know how

Reproduced with permission of Health Promotion England.

Reproduced here are both sides of a leaflet produced by the Health Education Authority encouraging people to protect themselves against sunlight. It incorporates several elements described in this section, and in Chapter 1.

- **Credibility of the communicator:** the Yale Model of Communication stresses the importance of a credible source of information; if this leaflet was produced by a sunscreen manufacturer, people may take its message with a pinch of salt. However, the name Health Education Authority implies that the advice comes from an impartial government agency, and the use of the word 'authority' gives more weight to the advice in the leaflet.
- **Fear arousal:** this is necessary in order to get people to perceive a threat (see the sections describing the Health Belief Model and the Theory of Planned Behaviour in Chapter 1, pages 11–15). This leaflet uses mild fear arousal, by stressing the connection between sunburn and skin cancer, and by drawing attention to other bad effects of too much sun (for example, wrinkles, heat stroke). However, it avoids strong fear arousal, which could be achieved by, for instance, showing graphic images of people suffering from skin cancer.
- **Perceived susceptibility:** getting people to realize that a condition is serious is not sufficient in order for them to perceive a threat; they also have to accept that they are

personally susceptible. This leaflet attempts to convince people of this by pointing out how common skin cancer is, and by listing factors that can make people especially at risk (for example, pale skin, a family history of skin cancer and so on). The fact that the leaflet is written in the second person (that is, using words like 'you' and 'your') also increases perceived susceptibility.

- **Self-efficacy:** in order to change behaviour, it is important for the individual to believe in his or her ability to do so. This leaflet tries to make it seem easy to protect oneself from the sun by clearly and simply setting out a range of protective measures.

- **Costs versus benefits:** both the Health Belief Model and the Theory of Planned Behaviour incorporate the notion that, before a person chooses to modify his or her behaviour, he or she has to be convinced that it is worthwhile doing so – that is, that changing one's behaviour will be effective in protecting oneself. There are two phrases in this leaflet that stress this: 'Most cases of skin cancer could be easily prevented' and 'If skin cancers are treated early, they should cause you no further problems'. This last phrase is contained in a section that describes how to recognize the early signs of skin cancer, showing that the leaflet focuses on **secondary** as well as on **primary health promotion**.

- **Other elements:** the Yale Model of Communication mentions the effectiveness of involving the audience, which this leaflet does not do, and also it gives its health message very explicitly, which is less effective if the message is simple or the audience well-informed; this may be because the leaflet is not aimed at people who are already aware of the risks of sunburn. An important feature of the Theory of Planned Behaviour is **subjective norm**, made up of people's perceptions about other people's attitudes to the behaviour, and their motivation to conform – this leaflet does address this aspect.

Summary

- The 'Sun know how' leaflet produced by the Health Education Authority is carefully designed to take into account many of the research findings that apply to health promotion messages.

Questions

1 Consider each sentence of the leaflet separately, and describe which psychological theories or findings it is related to.

2 Do you think this leaflet would be effective in modifying people's behaviour, including your own?

The idea that exercise helps slow down the ageing process is further supported by research carried out by DeVries (1977) (cited in Sheridan and Radmacher, 1992, p. 187), which shows that not only can many of the negative physical characteristics of ageing be reversed through exercise, but also that these characteristics can be produced in young people by keeping them in bed for several weeks. Ogden (1986) suggests the following possible explanations for how exercise can help people lead longer, healthier lives:

- It helps to reduce blood pressure.
- It helps people avoid being overweight or obese.
- It seems to reduce the damaging effects of diabetes.
- It protects against osteoporosis and thinning bones.
- It reduces coronary heart disease.

There is not the scope in this book to examine in detail the relationship between exercise and physiological improvements to health; research in this field is carried out by medical professionals rather than health psychologists. Once it has been established that exercise improves health, psychologists need to determine how best to persuade people to take more exercise, and the findings related to health promotion described earlier in this chapter are relevant to this question. However, psychologists are also interested in whether exercise has mental as well as physical benefits.

Psychological benefits of exercise

There is a large body of evidence suggesting that people who exercise regularly tend to be less depressed and anxious, better at dealing with stressful situations and have higher self-esteem and self-confidence (Ogden, 1996). However, much of this research is **correlational**, meaning that it simply demonstrates a link between exercise and psychological benefits, and does not show that exercise actually **causes** the benefits; it may be the case that people who are less depressed to begin with are consequently more likely to go out and take part in activities involving exercise.

An experimental study that attempts to demonstrate a causal relationship was carried out by McCann and Holmes (1984, cited in Ogden, 1996). They found a significant reduction in the symptoms of depression among female students who were made to take regular aerobic exercise over a period of ten weeks.

There are several different explanations of why exercise may have psychological benefits. For example, it has been shown that aerobic exercise encourages the production of **endorphins** in the brain. Endorphins act as natural opioids, reducing pain and making people feel less depressed (drugs such as morphine and heroin work by mimicking the action of endorphins). The production of endorphins as a result of exercise may explain the emotional 'high' that people report after periods of intense physical activity. Perhaps the psychological benefits of exercise arise directly out of the physical benefits; people feel happier if they are physically healthier. Or maybe the increased social contact that accompanies most forms of physical exercise has a beneficial psychological effect (see the section on social support in Chapter 4, pages 80–1). Finally, it may be the case that exercise leads to a feeling of physical competence and provides people with a greater feeling of self-efficacy and self-esteem.

Commentary

- Although exercise is generally considered to be a healthy thing to do, it can also be harmful. Exercise that is too strenuous can damage health, and so it is important for people to tailor their exercise regimes to their levels of fitness. More moderate exercise programmes also help to avoid certain injuries such as pulled muscles, tendonitis and shin splints. A factor to consider here is the individual's motivation for taking exercise; if the physical activity is being undertaken as part of his or her employment or in order to compete in a sport, for example, then the risk of injury is higher than if the exercise is specifically aimed at improving health and fitness.

- In principle, exercise is a cheap health protective behaviour, available to people from all socioeconomic classes; it does not cost anything to go for a walk or to do a few push-ups. However, in practice, people need to find time and space to exercise, and many types of exercise cost money, for equipment, tuition or access to facilities. Health campaigns aimed at persuading people to take more exercise need to take this factor into account.

Nutrition

Most people find foods that are high in fat or in sugar particularly tasty; this makes evolutionary sense because high calorie foods are very useful for hunter-gatherers, and their tastiness provides a strong motivation to seek them out. In today's world, food is plentiful for many people (although

The type of exercise that people can take is affected by their economic circumstances.

malnutrition and starvation is still distressingly common), and our taste for sweet and fatty food leads to many people over-eating.

An unhealthy diet does not just consist of eating too much, or too little, but can also involve eating the wrong kinds of food. It is generally accepted that too much salt or not enough roughage is bad for you, but some people believe that non-organic food, for example, is also harmful. Perhaps the closest link between diet and health is made by the ancient Indian practice of ayurveda. Apart from general rules about how to eat healthily (for example, not eating re-heated food, not filling one's stomach completely during a meal, not talking, watching TV or reading while eating), this system suggests a very specific diet tailored to an individual's body type, his or her current state of health and even the time of year.

There is a great deal of evidence that diets high in fat, salt and sugar, and low in fibre, vitamins and minerals lead directly to ill health – particularly coronary heart disease, cancer and strokes. The physiological relationship between certain diets and specific medical conditions is beyond the scope of this book. Of interest to health psychologists, though, are possible explanations as to why people eat in ways that harm their health. By understanding the reasons that underlie poor diets, health promotion professionals may be able to persuade people to eat in a more healthy manner.

Genetic theories

As mentioned earlier (see page 33), it seems sensible to assume that, through a process of evolution, human beings have become genetically pre-programmed to crave high calorie food. However, this does not explain why only some people over-eat. Twin and adoption studies seem to suggest a strong genetic predisposition to obesity, perhaps because **metabolic rate** (that is, how much energy people require to survive) and the number of **fat cells** in our bodies are partially inherited.

However, except for very rare conditions, genetic inheritance does not determine behaviour. In other words, if an individual is at risk of obesity due to his or her nature then, by being made aware of this, he or she can be particularly careful about diet. This does mean, though, that staying at a healthy weight is much easier for some people than for others and it is perhaps unfair to attribute obesity to laziness or lack of will power. The implication of assuming that an individual has little behavioural control over his

or her weight is that weight loss treatment has to be imposed on the individual, and there have been some dramatic examples of individuals being forced, using a range of coercive techniques, to eat low calorie diets.

Behaviourist theories

The three behaviourist theories described in Chapter 1 (see pages 8–9) can be applied to overeating. Classical conditioning, for example, might explain the phenomenon of **comfort eating**. In operant conditioning, people behave in ways that are reinforced; the trouble with unhealthy food is that it is often very rewarding in the short term (that is, delicious) and the costs (that is, health problems) do not occur immediately. The example used to illustrate the **social learning** theory was that of young women with eating disorders (see RLA 2, page 17), but observation and imitation can also encourage people to eat more; in fact, adverts for processed food are specifically designed to do this. The implications for health promotion of these theories are:

- undermine any associations that have been made as a result of past experience between unhealthy food and comforting or positive feelings.
- attempt to make healthy food as rewarding to eat as unhealthy food and, failing this, encourage people to **delay gratification** – that is, to forego an immediate pleasant experience in the hope that it will result in a greater reward in the long run.
- provide positive role models for people and regulate the food industry so that advertising does not make false claims about the health implications of the foods it is selling.

Cognitive theories

A cognitive approach to diet would assume that eating behaviour is the outcome of rational decisions. According to the Health Belief Model, people must perceive a threat in order to decide to modify their behaviour, then need to believe that the change has more benefits than costs.

Similarly, one component of the Theory of Planned Behaviour is the individual's attitude towards the behaviour. This means that, in order to persuade people to eat a healthier diet, they need to be convinced that their current diet is bad for them, and that the health improvements associated with a new diet are worth the trouble, and expense, of changing.

The Theory of Planned Behaviour also mentions subjective norm, and health promotion campaigns have sometimes tried to get individuals to change diet on the grounds that their loved ones will approve.

The final component of the Theory of Planned Behaviour is perceived behavioural control; the implications of this are that health promotion campaigns aimed at healthy eating need to persuade individuals that it is they who are responsible for what they eat (internal locus of control), and that they have the skills and knowledge to modify their own diets if they choose to do so (self-efficacy).

Commentary

- One of the difficulties in persuading people to eat well is that ideas about exactly what types of food constitute a healthy diet tend to vary. Doctors and nutritionists do not always agree among themselves about whether certain foods are good or bad and this means that individuals who wish to avoid the issue can use this disagreement as an excuse for not making an effort to modify their diets.
- As with exercise, eating a healthy diet can be more expensive and time consuming. In the 1980s, Edwina Currie, who was then a Conservative Government Health Minister, caused a great deal of offence by suggesting that the higher rate of coronary heart disease in the north of England could be dealt with by people eating fewer chips; the average income of people in the North of England is significantly lower than in the South.

Health promotion programmes

There are many different settings in which health promotion can take place – for example, in schools, in workplaces, in local communities, in hospitals and other health care places or in the mass media. The characteristics of a successful health promotion programme will depend largely on its setting. This section looks at specific examples of health promotion programmes in three different settings:

- the workplace
- schools
- the community.

Health promotion in the workplace

There are two reasons why the workplace is a useful setting for health promotion: first, it is a good way to gain access to a large captive audience and, second, many behaviours linked to ill health occur within the workplace. This is underlined by the following figures published by the Health Education Authority in 1997 (cited in Naidoo and Wills, 2000, p. 266):

- 18% of deaths in the UK are work-related
- 6% of adults suffer ill health associated with work
- 115 million working days are lost every year in the UK as a result of work-related illness or injury (including stress-related illness).

There are several ways in which health promotion can occur within the workplace – including:

- adequate health and safety policies (this is discussed in more detail on page 44)
- occupational health – first aid and medical treatment, health screening
- health education – advice about healthy lifestyles
- provision of facilities and services such as gyms, stress counselling and so on
- creating a healthier environment – for example, by providing a healthy diet in the canteen or by banning smoking.

RLA 4 looks at an example of the last of these – banning smoking in the workplace.

Real Life Application 4: Workplace smoking bans

This RLA is based on a study carried out by Parry *et al* (2000) in which they evaluate a smoking ban implemented at a Scottish university in 1997. At first sight, it seems reasonable to ban smoking from public places: it makes it harder for smokers to smoke, meaning that they may cut down on their daily cigarettes; it protects non-smokers from environmental tobacco smoke; and it keeps the place cleaner. Comments from non-smokers at the university seemed to back this up. They said:

… we should be much more concerned about air quality and not exposing non-smokers to carcinogenic fumes

… the university should do nothing to make life easier for those who want to inflict toxins on people around them and who have no choice but to breathe in their effluent.

An alternative to banning smoking completely is to create dedicated smoking areas, but this is also unpopular among non-smokers, who said things like:

... I see no reason why the university should be forced to provide dedicated areas, and reducing smoking classes are a huge waste of valuable resources.

Consequently, the university implemented a policy of a complete smoking ban – a policy that is accepted by many workplaces and colleges around the country. The ban seemed to be accepted by university staff, and led to some reduction in levels of smoking and a reduction of environmental tobacco smoke inside the buildings. However, the smoking ban also led to a number of unintended consequences:

- environmental tobacco smoke shifted from inside the buildings to just outside, as smokers congregated around the entrances
- smokers at the university became more visible and gained a higher profile
- there was an accumulation of smoking debris in certain areas outside the buildings
- sympathy for smokers actually increased as they were perceived to be discriminated against.

The authors conclude that, while smoking bans are successful in reducing smoke pollution in workplaces, they do not really solve the problem of smoking at all. Banning smoking from inside buildings simply shifts the problem elsewhere (in fact, many smokers reported that they had started smoking more outside working hours as a result of the ban). The authors do not support the idea of designated smoking areas on the grounds that it is difficult to ensure that smoke pollution does not leak out from such areas, and that this, while appearing to condone smoking, also serves to ghettoize smokers and render them invisible. They recognize that the main aim of smoking bans is to reduce environmental tobacco smoke, but argue that the only long-term solution to the problem is to provide help for smokers to cut down or quit smoking.

Adapted from Parry *et al*, 2000.

Summary

- The problems of environmental tobacco smoke means that most workplaces do not allow people to smoke where they want.
- Rather than provide designated smoking areas, the university implemented a complete smoking ban.
- Although smoking was reduced at work, there were a number of unintended consequences that undermined the effectiveness of the ban.
- The authors conclude that the only long-term solution to smoking at work is to provide help for smokers to give up.

Questions

1 What problems occur if smoking is allowed in an institution such as a university?

2 What are the side-effects of a complete smoking ban?

3 What are the alternatives to a complete smoking ban?

4 What is the policy on smoking at your college/workplace, and do you think it is effective?

Health promotion in schools

Many health-related behaviours become habitual at a fairly young age, and teenagers in particular begin to behave in ways that can cause serious problems later on. For example, very few people take up cigarette smoking if they have not already done so by the age of eighteen, and young people are particularly vulnerable to the dangers of substance misuse and unsafe sex. Therefore, it makes sense to start health education as early as possible, and schools seem to be an ideal setting for this: there is a captive audience, already studying in an educational environment, and teachers can be specifically trained to provide high quality health education. In fact, various government publications (ranging from National Curriculum subject orders to the non-statutory framework for teaching Personal, Social and Health Education) suggest that the following topics could be taught in schools:

- substance use and misuse
- sex education
- family life education

- safety
- health-related exercise
- food and nutrition
- personal hygiene
- environmental aspects
- psychological aspects.

Unfortunately, the practice of health promotion in schools does not always match up to its good intentions, and many young people are critical of the health education they receive. A detailed discussion of the purposes and techniques of school health education is beyond the scope of this book, but it is a very useful exercise for the reader to recall specific examples of health education that he or she has personally experienced, and to analyse it with respect to the issues raised in this chapter.

Health promotion in the community

Community-based health promotion is based on the assumption that social and environmental factors play an important role in people's health, and that it is possible to modify social structures in ways that encourage people to lead healthier lives. As made clear in Chapter 1 (see pages 22–3), the key environmental and social change needed to improve health is reducing poverty, as negative social conditions are the most important contributors to ill health. However, this involves political activity that is beyond the scope of most health promotion professionals, who consequently attempt to make whatever changes they can within the current sociopolitical climate. Specific examples of health promotion in the community include:

- local environmental campaigning (for example, against road pollution, for safer roads and more green spaces)
- 'social' campaigning (for example, for better quality housing and adequate policing against racist attacks)
- improving local services (for example, adequate provision of public transport, shops, post offices, health services and community centres)
- improving the social environment (for example, encouraging community or voluntary organizations and self-help groups)
- encouraging specific behaviour (for example, getting shops to ask for ID before selling cigarettes to young people and encouraging people to check up on elderly neighbours).

Substance use

The term **substance use** refers to the ingestion by various means of specific chemicals aimed at altering one's physical or mental state. This section focuses on alcohol and tobacco, with some reference to the use of illegal drugs. Different societies throughout history and around the world have been very interested in the use of mind-altering chemicals, and these have had very positive as well as very negative social, cultural and health implications. For the individual user, also, there are both positive and negative effects of use, and these need to be considered from a psychological perspective in order to understand why people use (and in particular misuse) these substances and how substance misuse can be prevented or alleviated.

Physiological effects of substances

There are many reasons why people use substances such as tobacco and alcohol. One is the positive **physiological** effects of these substances.

At the time when cigarette smoking was at its peak (in the 1950s and 1960s) people were largely ignorant of the long-term physical side effects of smoking (see page 37), and people smoked (and still do) partly because of the pleasurable physiological effects. **Nicotine** is the addictive chemical in cigarettes, and it is this that produces rapid and strong effects. When a person smokes, the nicotine is absorbed very quickly into the blood stream through the membranes in the mouth, throat and lungs. It is carried to the brain where it triggers the release of a number of chemicals, including **acetylcholine** and **norepinephrine**, which have the effect of enhancing concentration and alertness, and increasing pleasurable feelings. These chemicals also reduce feelings of tension and anxiety (Sarafino, 1994).

Alcohol, like nicotine, also produces particular physiological effects in the body. Alcohol affects the **central nervous system**, and depending on the amount of alcohol consumed, this effect can range from physical relaxation and a reduction in feelings of anxiety, to serious impairment in judgement and co-ordination. Large amounts of alcohol consumed in a short space of time can paralyse vital reflexes and cause death. However, most people use alcohol because of its relaxing effect. Alcohol reduces the production of **catecholamine** (a chemical that produces a sense of arousal and is associated with stress). More recently, alcohol has also been shown to increase the production of substances in the bloodstream that protect the blood vessels from cholesterol.

Psychoactive drugs have many and various physiological effects – for example, the effect of narcotics such as heroin on chemicals in the brain can cause feelings of euphoria and intense well-being. Stimulants such as cocaine produce physiological and psychological arousal that gives feelings of confidence and well being, and hallucinogens such as marijuana produce distortions in perception and feelings of relaxation.

In the long term, the misuse of all these substances is likely to have negative physiological consequences. The long-term physiological effects of smoking tobacco are now well known. Smoking is implicated in coronary heart disease and various types of cancers – including lung, throat and bowel. The life expectancy of smokers is shorter than for non-smokers.

The physiological effects of long-term misuse of alcohol are also clear – alcohol misuse can increase the chance of developing cirrhosis of the liver, and also certain cancers such as pancreatic and liver cancers. Additionally, alcohol increases the likelihood of accidents – caused, for example, by drink-driving.

Psychoactive drugs can cause physical harm to the body – for example, cocaine can affect the cardiovascular system by raising blood pressure and causing the heart to beat very fast. It can also destroy membranes in the nose. Drug use is a factor in many road accidents, and it is now well known that babies can be born addicted to drugs such as heroin and cocaine if their mothers used them during pregnancy, because drugs such as these can cross the placenta.

When does 'use' become 'misuse'?

Most people will have tried alcohol and tobacco at some stage in their lives, and many will also have tried psychoactive drugs. For the majority, the use of these substances never becomes a problem.

Many people drink regularly, and moderate consumption of alcohol (within government guidelines – currently 21 units per week for men and 14 units per week for women) may actually enhance health rather than detract from it. There is evidence to suggest that these drinkers have lower morbidity and mortality rates than heavy drinkers and those who abstain altogether (Rimm *et al*, 1991). The effects of the number of cigarettes smoked is less clear,

although the more a person smokes, the more dangerous it becomes. A person can be addicted to nicotine even if he or she smokes only a few cigarettes a day.

In trying to understand why people smoke, drink or take drugs it is important to understand when use becomes 'misuse' or addiction, and to understand what we mean by addiction.

Addiction

People are sometimes described as having 'addictive' personalities, and researchers now look at the ways in which people can become addicted to certain types of behaviours – gambling or sex, for example – as well as to certain types of substance. But how do we define 'addiction'? Sarafino gives a helpful definition that is simple and clear, and also distinguishes between physical and psychological addiction.

> *Addiction is a condition, produced by repeated consumption of a natural or synthetic substance, in which the person becomes physically and psychologically dependent on the substance (1994, p. 206).*

Physical dependence is the condition in which the substance has become incorporated into the normal physiological functioning of the body. It is associated with tolerance of the substance (that is, users need to take more and more in order to get the same effect), and with withdrawal symptoms (that is, uncomfortable or painful physical feelings if users stop taking the substance or cut down). Some substances, such as nicotine and heroin, create physical dependence more easily than others.

Psychological dependence is the condition in which people come to rely on a substance because they enjoy the effect it has on them, without necessarily being physically dependent on it. Some substances such as marijuana may have this effect.

But when is use seen as misuse? Often this is determined by whether a person is addicted to a substance or not. Rosenhan and Seligman (1984) suggest that three factors indicate what they call substance abuse:

- pathological use and an inability to stop
- the use has problematic effects on the person's life – with their work, family or friends
- the pathological use lasts for at least one month.

The DSM IV (the current diagnostic manual of the American Psychiatric Association) classifies alcohol abuse as a maladaptive drinking pattern described in much the same way as Rosenhan and Seligman describe substance abuse in general. Those who abuse alcohol are diagnosed on the basis of one of the following:

- recurrent drinking in spite of its effect on personal obligations
- continued drinking in spite of legal or personal problems associated with its use
- recurrent drinking in situations where this is dangerous.

Ogden (1996) gives an interesting review of attitudes to alcohol use and addiction over time, and how these have changed in relation to prevailing social values. She argues that in the seventeenth century there was a **'moral' model** in relation to alcohol use. At this time alcohol was often considered to be safer than water, and its use was widespread. Alongside this, attitudes towards human behaviour reflected ideas about free choice, and so if people used or misused alcohol it was seen as a result of their own free will. Alcoholism was therefore regarded as a punishable behaviour, not a behaviour that needed treatment, as individuals were responsible for their own actions.

By the nineteenth century attitudes had changed, and what Ogden refers to as the **'first disease concept'** of addiction was developed. This model was reflected in the attitudes of the Temperance Movement, and Prohibition in the USA. In this model the blame lay with alcohol itself, and it was seen as an addictive substance to which alcoholics could succumb and which would make them ill. This is a kind of medical approach to addiction, and one in which alcoholism was seen as an illness that needed treatment.

By the beginning of the twentieth century this model shifted slightly in its attitude to alcohol, which once again became an acceptable substance. This model became known as the **'second disease concept'**, in which the behaviour of the few individuals who became addicted was once again seen as the problem, rather than the alcohol itself. However, as in the 'first disease concept' alcoholism was regarded as an illness that needed treatment and support.

Since the 1970s attitudes and ideas have shifted again, with a move away from the medical approach and a move towards a psychosocial approach related to **social learning theory**. In this model addictions are being seen, at least in part, as learned behaviours. This approach appears to lean towards a notion of misuse rather than addiction.

Ogden (1996) compares the 'second disease concept' with the 'social learning' perspective, and draws some interesting comparisons.

The second disease concept argues that:

- addictions are discrete – a person is either addicted or not
- addictions are illnesses
- the individual is seen as the problem
- the addiction cannot be reversed
- treatment requires total abstinence.

Social learning theory argues that:

- addictive behaviours are learned
- addictive behaviours can be unlearned
- addictive behaviours are not discrete – but lie on a continuum
- addictive behaviours are no different from other behaviours, and treatment involves abstinence or unlearning the behaviour.

These explanations will be examined in relation to types of prevention and alleviation (on pages 42–4).

Commentary

Ogden's summary of the social learning approach to addiction highlights some of the problems with the second disease concept. It is very difficult to achieve life long abstinence, so this method of treatment may not be effective. Furthermore, because it is difficult to achieve abstinence, those attempting it may be setting themselves up to fail, so end up with a self-fulfilling prophecy.

Why people misuse substances

There are many reasons why people start and continue to misuse substances, and these reasons can be grouped into three categories:

- physical
- psychological
- social and environmental.

Most clinicians now recognize that it is a combination of these factors that has an overall effect on the likelihood of misuse by an individual.

Physical factors affecting misuse

There is evidence to suggest that genetic factors may have an influence over substance misuse. The effects of both alcohol and nicotine are influenced by genetic factors to some degree. Family, adoption and twin studies have shown that there may be a link to alcoholism (Sayette and Hufford, 1997). Genetic variation in the function of dopamine receptors and liver enzymes that metabolize nicotine may influence whether a person is more or less vulnerable to nicotine addiction (Moolchan *et al*, 2000). RLA 5 considers the influence of genetic inheritance on alcoholism.

Real Life Application 5:
A gene for alcoholism?

There is some debate as to whether there is a gene for alcoholism. Certainly the tendency to abuse alcohol sometimes runs in families, but whether or not this is caused by an identifiable gene or whether this behaviour is the result of social learning is still open to question.

Some studies seem to suggest that there is a genetic predisposition to alcohol abuse. Recent American research into genetics and behaviour has looked at people's tendency to do things 'just for kicks'. It has been found that this type of behaviour, characterized by 'impulsiveness and excitability', is more common in people who have a certain gene that controls a particular receptor for dopamine in the brain. People with a different form of the same gene whose receptors are perhaps less sensitive to dopamine are more 'reflective and orderly'. If this is true then perhaps people who become alcoholics have the gene that encourages them to seek out new and stimulating experiences.

Other studies, however, argue that there is no such gene, and that alcohol abuse has many social and environmental causes.

Adapted from Luisa Dillner, 'Is it all in the genes?', *The Guardian*, 16 January 1996.

Summary

- It is still unclear whether there is a genetic predisposition to alcohol abuse. Some studies suggest that there is a genetic link, while others believe it has more to do with the environment.

Questions

1 How important do you think genes are in shaping a person's behaviour in this way?

2 What other factors might also be important?

Commentary

The obvious problem with the approach in RLA 5 is that it is reductionist to assume that genetic factors are the root cause of an alcoholic's problems. While there may be a genetic predisposition, there is a range of factors that may cause someone to misuse alcohol (including psychological and social factors, which are discussed in the text that follows).

Psychological factors affecting misuse

When looking at psychological factors that affect the use of cigarettes, alcohol and drugs, it is useful to refer to the models of health behaviour discussed in Chapter 1. The Theory of Planned Behaviour (see pages 13–15), for example, can be used to understand the cognitive factors that may contribute to a person starting, continuing or stopping smoking. If the theory is applied to an individual who wanted to give up smoking, then it might explain his or her intention in the following ways.

A positive attitude to the behaviour would be that the individual knows that cigarettes can cause health problems, that s/he may well develop such problems if s/he carries on smoking, and giving up smoking will be effective in protecting against these problems. A positive subjective norm would involve the knowledge that the individual's friends want him or her to stop smoking, and the individual caring about what his or her friends think. A positive sense of behavioural control may come from the knowledge that he or she can already do without cigarettes in the presence of these friends who do not smoke. The Theory of Planned Behaviour predicts that if all of these positive components are in place, the individual is more likely to decide to give up smoking.

However, the beneficial effects that adolescents, in particular, associate with smoking, drinking and taking drugs are important in explaining the initial use of these substances at this time. One area that has recently been the focus of research is risk-taking behaviour. Adolescence is the first time that young people have the opportunity to take risks as a mark of their growing independence. Involvement in the use of substances such as marijuana, tobacco and alcohol are seen to promote a person's sense of independence and maturity, and enhance their own self-image (Moolchan *et al*, 2000).

Peer pressure is also an important influence. A longitudinal study conducted in America showed that an important indicator of high school students' moving from trial to use of cigarettes was their friends' smoking and approval and cigarettes being offered to them by friends (Robinson *et al*, 1997).

Some studies suggest that personality traits may indicate a likelihood that a person will smoke, misuse alcohol or take drugs. Sensation-seeking personality types and impulsiveness are traits thought to relate to alcoholism (Sayette and Hufford, 1997).

One of the benefits of smoking that many adults report is improved concentration. It is well documented that withdrawal from nicotine reduces concentration levels and impairs other areas of cognitive functioning, so it may well be that these feelings are reported because addiction causes these symptoms if the level of nicotine in the blood stream is not maintained.

Many of the reasons why people become addicted to various substances can be related to classical conditioning, operant conditioning and social learning theory (see pages 8–9). The idea that, at least in part, addictions are learnt is one that has already been mentioned earlier. Many studies have confirmed this.

- An example of alcohol use being reinforced by classical conditioning is the way in which people learn to associate drinking with having a good time, or celebrating something.
- In relation to operant conditioning people drink alcohol, for example, to increase pleasant feelings (positive reinforcement), and to decrease unpleasant feelings (negative reinforcement).
- An example of social learning is the way in which people often drink because it is seen as an acceptable behaviour by their friends and family. Children often model their behaviour on adults, and studies show that children of parents who smoke are twice as likely to do the same themselves as the children of parents who do not. Adolescents for whom alcohol becomes a problem are also likely to have parents who drink moderately to heavily themselves (Orford and Velleman, 1991).

Another important reason why people may become addicted has to do with ego defence mechanisms.

For some people, addiction to a substance acts as a coping strategy and a defence against unwanted thoughts and feelings – for example, through suppression or denial (see page 10).

Social and environmental factors affecting misuse

Overall there has been a drop in the number of people who smoke in western countries. However, there has been a steady rise in the number of young women who smoke compared to young men. One finding about the differences between adolescent male and female smokers is that young women who smoke tend to be self-confident, socially skilled and rebellious, compared to young men who tend to be socially insecure (Clayton, 1991).

Perhaps one of the most important cultural factors that has had an impact on female smoking over the last 30 years is the desire to be slim (Moolchan *et al*, 2000). There are many ways in which our society, like many others, has promoted low body weight, and cigarette smoking is seen as a way to curb appetite. In the 1950s and 1960s women often advertised cigarettes, usually shown looking elegant and sophisticated. With changes in government legislation and a reduction in advertising of cigarettes, this reduced dramatically. However, in the last few years the number of fashion models shown smoking cigarettes has increased. Although these are not identified with a particular brand, it still sends messages to young women who are conscious of the way they look.

Drug and alcohol use do not appear to be a closely linked to gender differences, although fewer Black and Asian women smoke and drink than white women. This has been related to cultural values and religion.

As has already been discussed, age is a crucial factor in developing addictions. Most people who go on to become addicted to nicotine start smoking in secondary school. Drug addiction also tends to develop in adolescence or young adulthood, although this does vary according to the type of drug, and is linked to availability.

Availability and **social acceptability** cannot be overlooked as factors that shape substance use and misuse. Both cigarettes and alcohol are seen as perfectly acceptable in our society, and although there are age restrictions on when individuals can buy them (sixteen for cigarettes and eighteen for alcohol) drinking and smoking often start much younger than this.

Attitudes to drugs change over time – for

example, Ecstasy was legal until its use became widespread in the 1980s, and the use of marijuana is now being examined in the light of research that suggests it may relieve certain medical conditions.

Preventing and treating substance misuse

One of the points made earlier was that it is in adolescence that many of these addictive behaviours start. There are two ways of dealing with addiction – either to prevent it happening in the first place, or to treat it once it has happened. Most of the initiatives that are targeted at adolescents are directed at prevention rather than treatment.

Prevention

Most methods of prevention involve **public health interventions**. For children and adolescents these are often targeted through schools and colleges. For adults these occur more commonly through the workplace or in the doctor's surgery. Primary prevention programmes in schools often focus on the negative social aspects of smoking, such as bad breath and clothes that smell. Young people are more likely to be affected by this kind of message than one that is directed at the health risks, which seem remote to young people.

- **Workplace programmes:** in the workplace, strategies are usually directed at smoking, and usually involve no-smoking policies that ban smoking in all public areas. Smokers may be relegated to one smoking room that is open at particular times. However, studies on the effect of no-smoking policies show conflicting evidence: some show that there is a drop in overall smoking rates; other studies suggest that people smoke more outside office hours to compensate.

- **Government legislation:** government legislative interventions take several forms. Recently in Britain, and in a number of other European countries, the government has restricted tobacco advertising, and in some cases banned it altogether. These initiatives do seem to have reduced the number of smokers. The cost of smoking and drinking may also be prohibitive, especially for children. Ogden (1996) applies the Health Belief Model to this, by pointing out that the high price contributes to the perceived cost and is therefore an incentive to change behaviour. There are now also many places where smoking is banned, such as aeroplanes and tube trains. Some restaurants and bars operate no-smoking policies. It could be

argued that in the long run this will cause the cues to smoke and drink to be removed, but it might simply mean that people just go elsewhere instead (see RLA 4, page 35).

- **Doctor's surgeries:** these are effective places to promote health education messages, and people in waiting rooms are a passive audience for posters and leaflets. More important, perhaps, is the view of the doctor as a credible source of information. Doctors are usually talking to people who already smoke when they give advice on a personal level.

Treatment

There are a number of different ways to treat people who have a problem with a particular substance. There are various drug treatments for smokers and drug users that can help them to reduce and finally stop taking a substance, and there are various be-havioural and cognitive therapies that can be used.

- **Relapse prevention:** this approach to treatment recognizes that there is a risk of relapse and tries to focus on the situations in which this might occur. Rather than focusing on the lapse as a failure, this approach tries to help patients identify the situation that caused a lapse or might cause a lapse in the future, and to develop strategies to cope or to avoid the situation in the first place.

- **Skills training:** the ability to cope involves skills training in which a person is encouraged to develop his (or her) assertiveness, so that he develops strategies to refuse a drink or a cigarette, for example. People are also encouraged to use behavioural strategies such as chewing gum, or doing something in particular when they have a craving for alcohol or cigarettes. Skills training also encourages people to use support groups.

- **Self-help groups:** many alcoholics, drug users and smokers gain a great deal of social support (see page 81) from self-help groups such as Alcoholics Anonymous. These groups meet to discuss the experiences of those who are trying to abstain or control a dependence. Members can discuss their fears and get social support from other members, who can reassure and encourage them.

- **Aversion therapies:** aversion therapies involve trying to extinguish the behaviour by introducing unpleasant stimuli – for example, electric shocks or unpleasant pictures or films. Smokers are sometimes encouraged to smoke continuously as an aversive therapy. This is relatively effective, but cannot be used for all smokers.

- **Advice from doctors:** sometimes communicating a message in a simple way, but a way that comes from a credible source, can be very effective. Key Study 4 gives an example of a simple, but effective strategy used by a group of doctors to encourage people to give up smoking.

Commentary

- Specific treatments for people who misuse drugs can be classified according to the model of health promotion they adopt (see pages 26–7). For example, aversion therapies are related to the behaviour change model of health promotion, in that the therapist does what is best for the drug user and attempts to modify his or her behaviour accordingly, using a coercive technique. Skills training and advice from doctors, on the other hand, are related to the educational model of health promotion, in that drug users are given information and skills that could contribute to a successful decision to give up or cut down on their substance use.
- Different drug treatments are based on specific psychological theories or approaches. Aversion therapy, for example, is a direct application of classical conditioning (by attempting to create an association between the substance and an unpleasant response, such as pain or nausea). Another example concerns the social support received by drug users within self-help groups; this can serve to improve their sense of self-efficacy and therefore, according to the Theory of Planned Behaviour, increase the chances of them successfully giving up the substance.

KEY STUDY 4

Researchers: Russell, Wilson, Taylor and Baker (1979)

Aim: To assess the effectiveness of routine simple-but-firm advice to stop smoking being given by GPs to all their patients who smoke.

Method: During a four-week period, 28 GPs in 5 London practices targeted 2138 smokers who attended their surgeries. The smokers were allocated to 1 of 4 different conditions: group 1 were used as 'non-intervention' controls; group 2 were 'questionnaire-only' controls; group 3 (389 people) were advised by their GP to stop smoking; and group 4 (408 people) were advised by their GP, given a leaflet and told that they would be followed up some time later. It was possible to use follow-up data from 1884 patients after 1 month (88%), and 1567 after 1 year (73%).

Results: Marked differences in attitude were apparent almost immediately after the advice was given, both in the intention to stop smoking and in the motivation to do so. Most of the people who stopped smoking did so because of the advice. Motivation to stop was highest in the first month after the advice from the doctor, but was still an important factor shaping behaviour after 3 months. The cessation of smoking was most apparent in the group who had been given the leaflet as well as the advice. After 1 year the numbers who were still not smoking were 0.3% in group 1, 1.6% in group 2, 3.3% in group 3 and 5.1% in group 4. `

Conclusions: The results of the study after 1 year suggest that a GP who uses advice plus leaflets to enhance this advice will have a success rate of about 25 people who give up smoking each year. While this does not seem a huge number, if every GP in the country followed this routine the implication is that there would be more than half a million ex-smokers each year.

Commentary

The kind of approach described in Key Study 4 is based on three underlying cognitive theories about people's beliefs and motivations:

1 It is necessary to persuade people that they want to give up the drug-taking behaviour. This can be achieved by manipulating elements of the Health Belief Model (for example, increasing perceived threat, or decreasing perceived costs).
2 People have to be convinced that they are capable of

giving up, and this is achieved by increasing their sense of self-efficacy.

3 People have to believe that it is their own responsibility to give up, and this is achieved by encouraging them to have a more internal health locus of control.

- **Clinics:** these often adopt a number of different ways to treat patients at the same time, rather than using one particular approach. Lando (1977) developed a multistrategy approach that was used to stop people smoking: It used the following technique:

  – for one week, participants undergo six sessions of continuous smoking, lasting twenty-five minutes
  – then participants double their daily smoking rates overall for one week
  – participants stop smoking
  – they identify problems in trying to do this and develop strategies for dealing with these problems
  – they reward themselves if they have successfully stopped – they give themselves a treat, for example
  – they punish themselves if they lapse back into smoking – withdrawing a pleasure or giving money to a friend, for example.

This model appears to have success rates of above 70% over the six-month period following treatment. Treatment that involves more than one strategy to enable the person to give up or control their use of a substance does appear to be more effective than using one strategy on its own. However, there are still problems with this type of approach since relapse is always possible, especially when the support of therapists in a clinical setting comes to an end.

Commentary

- One of the most important issues in evaluating all these interventions is how effective they really are. While it may appear that fewer people smoke, misuse alcohol or take drugs, how are the figures measured? For example, self-report measures are unreliable in this area, as people often underestimate or lie about their use. This obviously makes accurate reporting very difficult.
- It is also difficult to measure the overall effect of a government programme compared to a specific treatment.

- With treatment programmes, physiological measures may be a more valid and reliable measure of adherence than self-report, but when the measurement is stopped will the people involved manage to maintain the abstinence?

Health and safety

Definitions, causes and factors affecting accidents

Accidents are a major cause of death and illness in Britain. Some groups are more vulnerable than others. Children, disabled people and old people are particularly vulnerable to accidents, and men are more likely to die from accidents than women. Accidents are the most common cause of death in people under 30 years of age.

Definitions

Pheasant defines an accident as ' …an unplanned, unforeseen or uncontrolled event – generally one which has unhappy consequences' (1991, p. 176). Accidents are usually caused by more than one factor. Pheasant argues that an accident may be caused by a combination of unlikely circumstances that cause an unexpected event.

A recent example of this, which had tragic consequences, was the series of circumstances that came together to cause the crash of the French Concorde just outside Charles de Gaulle Airport (Paris) in July 2000. The crash was caused by a piece of metal that punctured one of the tyres of the airplane. This sent shrapnel up into the wing, bursting the fuel tanks, which caused the fire. The small piece of metal had fallen off the fuselage of another plane that had taken off on the same runway minutes before Concorde. Runways at airports are inspected for debris several times a day. However, on this particular day another factor that may have precipitated the problem was that the morning inspection of the runway at Charles de Gaulle had been postponed because of a fire drill. Concorde had been flying for nearly 30 years with no fatalities, and in this one accident over 100 people were killed.

When an accident is as serious as this, or when it is on a large scale, it is sometimes referred to as a disaster or a catastrophe. Sometimes catastrophes are caused by what are known as 'acts of God' – natural disasters such as earthquakes or floods – but more often disasters are caused by human error or mechanical failure, as in the case of the Concorde crash. Even with mechanical failure, human error may be the cause because the equipment wasn't checked carefully enough or it was misused in some way. Pheasant argues that accidents are either caused by 'unsafe behaviours' or they are caused by 'unsafe systems' in the work place. With the former it becomes necessary to change the behaviour, and with the latter to change the system.

Roberts and Holly (1996) list what they call the 'basic causes' of accidents in hospital settings. These could also be applied to other workplaces.

- Inadequate work standards: risks can develop through a lack of training and supervision.

- Inadequate equipment or maintenance of equipment: inadequate or inadequately tested equipment increases the risk of accidents occurring.

- Abuse or misuse of equipment, or failure to check equipment: these can all cause harm. Roberts and Holly cite an example of a boy who suffered irreversible brain damage caused by a foreign body passing from an anaesthetic tube into his trachea and remaining there unnoticed, obstructing his airway for long enough to cause brain damage.

- Lack of knowledge: this could be how to use equipment safely and effectively, for example.

- Inadequate physical or mental capacity to do the job required: either because the person is physically unable, or because he or she may be drinking too much, or has some kind of mental illness.

- Mental or physical stress: this can make people vulnerable to accidents.

- Improper motivation: behaviour that puts other people in the workplace at risk. Roberts and Holly cite the case of Beverley Allitt, a nurse who was motivated to harm her patients rather than care for them. Another good example would be Dr Shipman who killed many of his elderly female patients.

Causes of accidents

Roberts and Holly go on to describe an example of the types of error health care professionals can make that can lead to accidents in a hospital setting. They describe situations in which what they call type I and type II errors can occur:

- **Type I errors** are due to 'omission' through a lack of knowledge about up-to-date or acceptable practice – for example, inadequate diagnosis or treatment being given in an Accident and Emergency department of a hospital.

- **Type II errors** occur through 'commission' – that is, when something is done that should not have been done. For example, a surgeon might take out the wrong kidney, or sever an artery through lack of concentration.

Some psychologists are interested in whether there are certain types of people who are more likely than others to have, or cause, accidents. One of the causes of accidents is sometimes related to what is often referred to as 'accident proneness'.

Personality and accident proneness

The concept of accident proneness is one that has been studied by many different psychologists. Greenwood and Woods studied the number of accidents that occurred in munitions factories in the First World War. They found that a relatively small group of people had a large number of accidents, concluding that this was due to more than chance alone (Pheasant, 1991). Some studies suggest that there are those who are 'risk takers' and those who are 'risk avoiders', and the basis of their behaviour is their overall attitudes to risk and danger and their view of the world. There are some people who seek out the adrenaline rush they experience from racing a car or parachuting out of a plane, and there are other people who would never engage in what they would consider to be such high-risk activities.

Studies of accidents in childhood sometimes use the term **'injury-prone personality'** to describe what happens to some children. Aggression is a predictor of injury in childhood, as is over-activity, and boys are three times as likely to be injured as girls (Pitts, 1996). However, Jaquess and Finney (1994) argue that economic deprivation is a more important indicator of the likelihood that a child will have an accident. They carried out a study in which they found no relationship between aggression or any other type of conduct disorder and accidents. They studied a group of economically deprived children who were participating in a summer camp scheme. They found that a disproportionately high number of the children who had accidents at the summer camp had also had accidents in the preceding year, and went on to have further accidents in the year after the summer camp. This kind of evidence is supported by statistics that show that, in general, children from more deprived backgrounds have a higher number of serious accidents than children from more affluent backgrounds.

The idea that some people are accident prone, or have accident-prone personalities, may be to do with psychological or physical characteristics, or the situation in which a person is working – for example, some people may be exposed to more risks than others. Pheasant (1991) describes accident proneness in terms of 'personal characteristics' – such as cognitive abilities and personality traits (for example, how extrovert a person is) – and 'transient states', which may be to do with illness or mood (something that affects the person, but is not lasting). He argues that extroverts, for example, have more accidents than introverts – perhaps because they are more impulsive. He also argues that accident-prone people may have problems with their cognitive abilities. For example, accident-prone drivers may have what is called '**field dependence**' – that is, they are not very good at extracting relevant information from a complicated perceptual field.

Psychoanalytic theory can be used to explain accident proneness as a form of withdrawal from a situation. Early studies, for example Hill and Trist (1953), have shown that accident-prone workers are also likely to have higher absenteeism than other workers, and these studies have drawn parallels between accident proneness and absenteeism, as both being examples of 'withdrawal behaviour'.

In terms of transient states, Pheasant (1991) cites the inevitable example of menstrual periods making women more accident prone. Illness is also likely to make people more accident prone, either because they are not physically capable of performing the tasks they are trying to do or because their illness makes them lose concentration. Similarly, mood can have an effect on concentration and a person's ability to think clearly and positively about what they are doing.

Reducing accidents and promoting safety behaviours

The Health of the Nation (1992) has specific targets to reduce accidents among the most vulnerable groups in the population by the year 2005. These targets aim to reduce death caused by accidents in:

- children under 15 by 33%

- those between 15 and 24 by 25%
- those over 65 by 33%.

Where young children are concerned, it is usually adults who have to take responsibility for promoting safe behaviours and preventing accidents. It is therefore adults who are targeted in health promotion and accident prevention campaigns rather than children. There are some messages that can be conveyed to children such as road safety – for example, the Green Cross Code in the 1970s, which is currently being conveyed by two cartoon hedgehogs. In contemporary society, however, there are fewer messages conveyed through the media, and more being taught in schools through Personal, Social and Health Education (PSE).

Wortel *et al* (1994) describe four safety behaviours that parents can engage in that prevent accidents among pre-school children. They list four important behaviours:

- educating the child about risks
- adequate supervision of the child
- making sure that the child's environment is safe
- giving first aid when an accident has happened.

Commentary

These behaviours may seem obvious in terms of child safety. However, these recommendations are not as straightforward as they seem. For example, it is difficult to make a child understand the nature of risk. It is almost impossible to ensure constant supervision, and also does not allow the child to explore the possibilities of its environment and learn from its mistakes. Making the environment safe is the most realistic option.

Some studies suggest that parents must understand the importance of their own role in eliminating risk and preventing accidents. In their survey, Langley and Silva (1982) found that only 39% of parents whose child had had an accident in the pre-school period changed their behaviour to prevent further accidents. Most of the parents who did not change their behaviour did not feel that it was possible to prevent the accident.

Commentary

The problem with an approach that focuses on the role of the parent is that it lays blame on these parents, instead of recognizing the need for a safe environment to be provided for everyone. For example, if we recognize that children who grow up in deprived homes are more likely to have accidents than those who do not,

Real Life Application 6:
The use of cycle helmets

A number of recent studies have looked at initiatives to encourage safe behaviour in children and adults alike, such as laws to make the use of seat belts compulsory for everyone. In her chapter on accidents and injuries, Pitts (1996) reviews recent studies on the promotion of the use of cycle helmets in various parts of the world. In a recent study in Maryland (USA), the use of cycle helmets was compared in three counties: one in which a law had been passed in 1990 making it mandatory for everyone under the age of 16 to wear an approved helmet; one in which publicity about proposed legislation was widespread, and one in which there were no laws or publicity.

Using self-report measures, the increase in helmet use rose from 11.4% to 37.5%, 8.4% to 12.6% and 6.7% to 11.1% respectively. Observations of the use of cycle helmets in the three counties found slightly different increases: from 4% to 47%, 8% to 19%, and in the county with no laws or publicity, there was a decrease during the period of survey. There is an obvious effect of legislation and campaigns.

A second study that shows the importance of what is known as passive intervention (legislation) was carried out in Australia. In one state in Australia, after ten years of health promotion about the importance of cycle helmets, their use was made compulsory by the state government. There was an immediate increase in helmet use from 31% in March 1990 to 75% a year later. The number of cyclists killed from head injuries decreased by 48% in the first year, and by 70% in the second year after the legislation had come into effect.

Adapted from *The Psychology of Preventive Health*, 1996.

Summary

- There is evidence that passive intervention, such as legislation, can have a real effect on health behaviour.
- In the case of legislation to promote the use of cycle helmets, in all the cases cited this rose significantly after the legislation was introduced.

Questions

1 Using the Health Belief Model, explain why some people would decide not to wear cycle helmets

2 Using the Yale Model of Communication, design a poster aimed at encouraging people to wear cycle helmets

3 Are self-report measures a valid way of getting results in the studies cited by Pitts?

then we often lay the blame for that statistic on negligent parents, rather than looking at the environment in which these parents are forced to bring up their children – in high-rise flats or on housing estates near main roads, for example.

RLA 6 explains the way in which the promotion of safe behaviours can be more effective if laws are passed to support these initiatives.

The workplace is one of the obvious targets for accident prevention campaigns and the promotion of safe behaviours. Some risk is unavoidable in certain jobs – for example, in occupations such as fire-fighting, deep-sea diving and fishing at sea, there is an inevitable risk that goes with the job. However, where possible these risks are minimized.

Oborne (1982) (cited in Pitts, 1996) uses a learning theory approach to understanding safety. He argues that often safety routines and practices take a lot of time, and that these behaviours are less likely to be reinforced than behaviours that are often quicker and easier, although more risky. It is useful therefore to focus on ways of making safe behaviours easier, and less time consuming to perform.

Pitts (1996) argues that there is now agreement in the literature on safety about how to try to prevent accidents in the workplace. She lists the following actions as the most important:

- to eliminate the hazards from the workplace
- to remove the individual from exposure
- to isolate the hazard
- workers can be issued with personal protection – such as protective clothing.

The emphasis in this model is that the action should be taken by the management of a company, rather than the individual working within it.

Commentary

These safety procedures are useful, but in the case of the first three actions they may not always be possible or practical.

Essay questions

1 Choose an example of health promotion material and analyse the content, describing which psychological techniques may have been used in its design.

2 Design an effective health promotion campaign aimed at a specific health related behaviour.

3 Describe and evaluate why people start and continue to misuse substances.

4 Describe and evaluate a number of programmes aimed at preventing or reducing substance misuse.

5 How can an understanding of the reasons why people have accidents help in reducing accidents and promoting safe behaviours?

3 Using medical services

This chapter is about the way in which patients use medical services, particularly in relation to their adherence to medical advice and their relationships with their doctors. The chapter also focuses on ways in which patients can be encouraged to adhere to the advice given to them, and examines the difficulties that both patients and doctors face in communicating effectively with each other. Real Life Applications that are considered are:

• RLA 7: Brain scan information leaflet

Adherence to medical advice

In the area of health care there is an increasing emphasis on self-care and personal responsibility for health. This is reflected in the need for patients to often understand and adhere to fairly complicated advice and information, and if necessary to treat themselves with a range of medicines. **Adherence**, or **compliance**, is defined as patients following the advice they are given by health-care professionals. This advice may involve adherence to medical regimes (such as taking pills), lifestyle changes (such as cutting down on foods high in fat or stopping smoking) or preventive measures (such as using condoms or wearing cycle helmets).

Ley (1997) argues that adherence often involves a number of behaviours, some of them quite complex, and that each one of these behaviours needs a decision about whether to adhere or not. Ley argues that even in the relatively simple example of taking medication, the patient has to obtain the medicine, start taking the appropriate dose, at appropriate intervals, and maintain this for the duration of the treatment. Sometimes a patient has to stop eating or drinking certain foods that might affect the treatment. This process in itself may encourage non-adherence.

Kent and Dalgleish (1996) describe a study in which many parents of children who were prescribed a ten-day course of penicillin for a streptococcal infection did not ensure that their children completed the treatment. The majority of the parents understood the diagnosis, were familiar with the medicine and knew how to obtain it. Despite the fact that the medication was free, the doctors were aware of the study and the families knew they would be followed up, by day three of the treatment 41%

of the children were still being given the penicillin, and by day six only 29% were being given it. This study very clearly illustrates the problem of non-adherence.

The costs associated with non-adherence can be high. The illness may be prolonged in the patient and he or she may need extra visits to the doctor. These are not the only costs, however, as the person may have a longer recovery period, might need more time off work or even require a stay in hospital. Non-adherence may lead to as much as 10%–20% of patients needing a second prescription, 5%–10% visiting their doctor for a second time, the same number needing extra days off work, and about 0.25%–1% needing hospitalization (Ley, 1997).

Measuring adherence

There are various ways to measure patient adherence. These can be divided into those that use **physical measures**, those that use **self-report measures**, and those that use **observational measures**.

Physical measures

Physical measures of measuring patient adherence include:

• blood tests
• urine tests
• outcomes – that is, an improvement in patient health, such as a drop in blood pressure.

Biochemical tests can determine whether the medication has been used recently, and in some cases how much has been used. Aherence can be measured in terms of outcomes, although people may get better even if they do not adhere.

Self-report and behavioural measures

Self-report and behavioural measures of patient adherence include:

- patient's reports
- devices that measure how many times the pill container is opened or measure out doses of medicine.

These are the most commonly used ways of measuring adherence. Doctors, especially those in general practice, are most likely to ask their patients whether they are sticking to their regime. Ley (1988) noted that while 78% of patients reported themselves to be adhering to their regime, more objective measures estimated the level of adherence to be closer to 46%.

Observational measures

Observational measures of patient adherence include:

- reports of friends and/or family
- the doctor's estimate
- attendance at the clinic or surgery.

Reports of family and friends can be helpful, as this participation usually means that the relatives or friends are offering social support alongside the observation. This should mean that the patient will receive encouragement to adhere to the advice they have been given.

In spite of the number of different ways to measure adherence it is very difficult to do this accurately. As was mentioned earlier some people may not adhere to a medical regime as fully as they say (or think) they do.

Commentary

- One of the difficulties with measuring adherence is the different ways in which patients might not adhere. These might vary from missing the occasional dose of medicine, to taking it at the wrong time or in the wrong amount, to deciding not to take it at all – for example, patients who are feeling better or who want to discover how they feel if they do not take it. (This is sometimes referred to as **rational non-adherence** – see page 51.)
- Physical measures, although reliable and objective, may not give the full picture. Although a blood or urine test might be able to determine whether a particular drug is present, and in what quantity (although it is not always possible to do this), it cannot always tell when the medication was taken or how regularly

it is taken. It is also time consuming and expensive to use this process in order to check adherence.

- Self-report measures are particularly problematic, for some of the reasons outlined earlier. People tend to over-report their adherence. This may be deliberate for a particular reason such as rational non-adherence, but often patients report what they think the doctor wants to hear or what they wish they were able to achieve. Sometimes patients' perception of what they are doing is inaccurate because they may not fully understand the method of treatment or the implications of not sticking to the regime they have been given. This method of checking on patient adherence (although one of the most widely used) is therefore very subjective and open to bias.
- Observational measures are reasonably valid, especially if they are used in conjunction with another method such as a patient self-report, or a blood or urine test. Often the person carrying out the observation helps to reinforce the treatment programme, and encourages the patient to adhere, so this is an effective method of measuring adherence and ensuring that adherence is maintained.
- According to research, one of the least valid ways of measuring adherence is to ask the doctor about their patient. While regular check-ups and attendance at clinic can be seen as reliable methods, doctors themselves often overestimate the adherence of their patients (Ley, 1997).

Why patients do not adhere

The reasons why patients do not adhere are complex and may be multidimensional. For example, the more complex the regime the less likely the patient is to adhere fully, and the more likely he or she is to make mistakes. The length of the treatment also has an effect; the longer the treatment the lower the adherence becomes. Some adherence involves the person making a change in a behaviour that is long standing, and this type of adherence also appears harder to maintain than adherence to a regime for taking medication.

Perceived threat

The Health Belief Model and the Theory of Planned Behaviour both stress the importance of perceived threat (made up of perceived seriousness and perceived susceptibility) in making health decisions. Kent and Dalgleish (1996) argue that it is not the ideas about seriousness on the part of the doctor that are important, it is the perceived seriousness of patients – in other words, the way in which they see their perceived illness does have a significant effect on the likelihood that they will adhere.

Kent and Dalgleish note that mothers who felt their children were susceptible to illness and who perceived this threat as serious were more likely to adhere to the treatment regime prescribed by their doctors and to keep appointments for check-ups than mothers who did not hold these beliefs. It is also true that patients' decisions to stop following advice are affected by how serious they perceive their illness to be. In studies where patients have been asked why they have stopped taking medication, the findings suggest that it is because they no longer feel ill and no longer consider their illness to be serious enough to need the medication. Caldwell *et al* (1970) also considered that this was connected with the patients' perceptions of their sick role – when they no longer felt ill the role no longer applied, and so they felt less inclined to follow the doctor's advice in the way that they did when they felt ill.

Rational non-adherence

Rational non-adherence is a term that refers to the deliberate act of not adhering for reasons the patient perceives as rational. Turk and Meichenbaum (1991) argue that patients might not take medication if they do not like the side effects, do not fully understand their treatment schedule or are not certain that the medicine is working.

One reason why people might not adhere is that they are concerned about the possible side effects of their treatment. Adherence decreases if the treatment seems worse than the illness, and this is particularly true if it affects cognitive functioning. Patients are prepared to suffer some physical discomfort as a side effect – nausea, for example – but are less willing to suffer problems with concentration, visual disturbance or sense of balance (Kent and Dalgleish, 1996).

Related to this is the idea that the diagnosis or treatment may be wrong. While the majority of patients have to trust their doctors, whom they accept must be more knowledgeable than themselves, doctors still need to convince their patients that they know what they are talking about (they must be credible), and that the treatment they are suggesting is the best one for that particular patient. Non-adherence may become a problem if the patient does believe in the effectiveness of the treatment offered.

Social support

Family circumstances may affect the likelihood that a person will adhere to medical advice. The level of social support a person receives from family and friends may be important in affecting how far they adhere to the medical regime given to them. Whether or not family members are living in the same house as the patient is also an indicator of how effective this will be (Kent and Dalgleish, 1996). When family members are present, they suggest that adherence is twice as good as when the patient is living alone.

Self-efficacy and conformity

Payne and Walker (1996) suggest that because people who have low self-esteem and low self-efficacy do not value their own ideas, they are more likely to adhere to medical advice because they value what the doctor tells them more than someone with high self-esteem. Similarly, a number of factors have been shown to be important in predicting the likelihood that a person will **conform** (or adhere), and one of these is if a person perceives that someone else has greater expertise than them (i.e. has a 'powerful others' locus of control, see page 16). This is often true of how people regard doctors.

Another factor that affects conformity is that people are more likely to conform if they have relatively little information on which to base their judgement; the less information, the higher the rate of conformity. This may seem counter-intuitive, but combined with some of the other factors already mentioned, Payne and Walker (1996), argue that many situations relating to patient adherence in health care are like this. Doctors tend to explain things to their patients on a 'need to know' basis, which leaves patients with little real knowledge about their condition or treatment.

Patient–practitioner relationships

It has been found that when patients believe their doctors to be concerned and interested in them, they are more likely to adhere to the medical advice given by a doctor. While status can have some effect, and the advice of a consultant might carry more weight than the advice of a less experienced doctor, it is still the individual approach of a particular doctor that is of the most importance to patients. This approach is reflected in the style of the doctor. Should doctors be distant and professional, or should they be more personal and friendly? There is no concrete answer to this question, as individuals prefer different doctoring styles, but it illustrates the idea that there are recognizable differences in style, that have been labelled by health psychologists as **doctor-centred**, **co-operative** and **patient-centred**:

- **Doctor-centred** relationships between patient and doctor revolve around the doctor being active and the patient being passive in the interactions that they have. The doctor is in charge and does not consider the patient's opinions in the decision making process about treatment.

- **Co-operative** (sometimes known as **guidance co-operative**) relationships between patient and doctor involve the doctor adapting the treatment to some degree to meet the wishes of the patient, but ultimately retaining the power and authority in the interaction.

- **Patient-centred** relationships between doctors and patients are more about a process of negotiation, where the patient can accept or reject the doctor's opinion, and is given the choice about how best to fit the available treatment options into his or her own lifestyle.

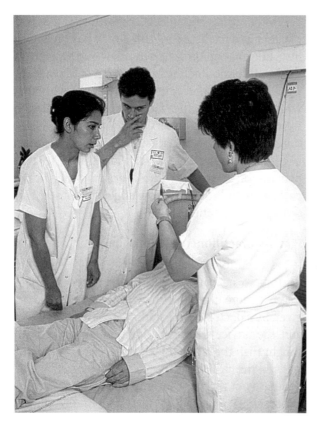

Doctor-centred treatment: the behaviour of the doctor may have an effect on the level of adherence.

Many studies show that a doctor-centred approach is the one that elicits the lowest level of adherence. Every patient has his or her preferred style, but problems arise most frequently when a doctor and patient have different styles and expectations.

The complexity of the message

The complexity of the instructions that patients have to follow can have a marked effect on their ability to understand and remember what they must do. One of the most straightforward problems for patients is remembering what doctors have told them to do, and it is important not to underestimate the importance of this simple problem, as it can seriously undermine adherence in spite of the best intentions a patient may have. Kent and Dalgleish (1996) cite studies that have found that patients forget what doctors have told them within a very short period of time. Different studies have found that patients can forget up to 50% of what they were told almost immediately after their consultation.

Improving adherence

At the beginning of this section it was suggested that whether or not a patient adheres to medical advice depends on a number of factors. It is difficult to differentiate between these factors in terms of their importance, as this will vary for each individual patient. However, there are some very simple and effective ways of improving patient adherence that seem to work for the majority of patients, whatever their circumstances. The two most obvious of these are to provide the support patients need, and to give them sufficient information (of the right kind) to enable them to adhere to the advice given. The second example involves the doctor–patient relationship in the process of conveying the information.

Social support

As was suggested earlier, the involvement of friends and family can encourage adherence. This can happen in a general way, perhaps with the friend sitting in on the consultation so that he or she is aware of the treatment programme; or the supporter can reinforce the treatment by actually being involved in the administration of the medication or monitoring the patient's use. If this is not possible, then support groups can play a very important role. Support groups for particular illnesses often encourage coping strategies, and can offer help and guidance about treatment and medication.

Providing information

It is common for doctors to under- or overestimate the amount of knowledge that patients possess. The consequences of this are that doctors either use jargon because they forget that their patients will not understand or to avoid having to explain information to the patient in simpler terms. Either way, patients are often left with a partial understanding of their treatment and how to administer it.

There is evidence to suggest that the more instructions a patient is given, the less he or she remembers. One way of dealing with this problem is to reduce the number of instructions and to make them as straightforward as possible. Another way of dealing with the problem of recall is to base instructions on the psychological theory of the primacy effect. The basis of this theory is that people remember best the information that they hear first. Ley (1988) suggests that in simplifying communication the doctor should take account of all these factors, as well as using repetition, stressing also the importance of adherence and making follow-up appointments.

Behavioural methods

Behavioural methods of encouraging patients to adhere include providing prompts and feedback for the patient – for example, in the form of labelled pill dispensers or those that make a noise at the time the medicine should be taken. Telephoned reminders can also be used, as can rewards for adherence. Rewards might take the form of being social or material – ranging from the approval of the doctor (social reinforcement) to a reward from the relative or support group, such as a trip or meal out (material reinforcement).

Ley (1997) lists a very straightforward set of guidelines for improving adherence, which includes a number of the examples given earlier:

- to make the treatment as simple and quick as possible
- to find out what individual patients' health beliefs are in order to evaluate whether the patients have an accurate perception of the seriousness of their condition and are aware of their susceptibility to the condition or the consequences of that condition
- to tailor the treatment to fit in with the patient's lifestyle
- to make sure patients are satisfied with the amount of information given about the treatment
- to make sure patients understand exactly what they must do and understand why the treatment is as it is
- to provide written guidelines for the treatment
- if possible, to involve a friend or family member in the process of treatment and adherence
- to provide support and back up, and sort out problems as they arise.

Commentary

- While all of the techniques described above may be very effective in improving adherence, there are certain practical implications that have to be considered. For example, some of the suggestions may take up additional time and money that doctors feel they do not have. However, improving adherence may save time and money in the long term, as patients will not need to visit the doctor as frequently.
- There are also implications for the training of doctors and other medical staff and, currently, medical students tend not to be trained in this area as effectively as they might be.

The patient–practitioner relationship

Underlying many of the factors affecting levels of adherence is the relationship between the doctor and his or her patient. This relationship can also affect other aspects of the treatment process, such as how satisfied patients feel with the way they are being treated and how effective the communication is between the patient and the doctor.

The way a doctor communicates with his or her patients can have an impact on how satisfied they are with the doctor and how much they understand their own conditions and treatment.

Interpersonal skills

Interpersonal skills are very important in shaping doctor–patient interactions. The information that is gained during the consultation is of vital importance in the diagnosis and treatment of any condition, since in order to carry out diagnostic testing a doctor must first understand the nature of the problem.

Studies that have looked at whether patients are happy with their treatment have focused on the process of the consultation. Some of these studies have discovered that whether or not patients are satisfied with their treatment relates to how the doctor communicates with them and whether, in the process of communicating, the patients feel they have been given enough information by the doctor, which has been explained sufficiently clearly. This has a great deal to do with the interpersonal skills of the doctor concerned.

According to Weinman (1997), many doctors have their own attitudes and beliefs about the patient's role in the consultation process. However, Weinman considers that one of the most important things the doctor must understand is the patient's own expectations. This is a difficult process and one that requires a great deal of sensitivity.

The interviewing technique that doctors develop is important because it has a lot to do with how satisfied the patient is with the consultation. Kent and Dalgleish (1996) argue that there are both **cognitive** and **emotional** components to a patient's satisfaction with their care.

- **Cognitive satisfaction** relates to how happy patients are with their understanding of the explanation of their diagnosis, treatment and prognosis.
- **Emotional satisfaction** is related to the doctor's non-verbal behaviour. The doctor's tone of voice is important in showing interest, and body posture can be equally important – patients want their doctor to appear interested and concerned by their condition.

Key Study 5 shows clearly the effect that doctor style can have on patient satisfaction. Although, in general, patients were satisfied with their consultations, the study has some interesting findings.

KEY STUDY 5

Researchers: Savage and Armstrong (1990)

Aim: To compare the effect of different types of communication styles of doctors on their patients' satisfaction with their consultation. These styles are described as 'directing' and 'sharing'. This research addresses the debate within medicine about the style of doctoring that suits patients best. Some doctors prefer the sharing style, while others still use the more traditional directing style, which is perceived to be more authoritarian and dominating.

Method: The study was carried out in an inner London general practice, where patients were free to chose which doctor they consulted. Some 359 participants were selected randomly, and from this original sample the results from 200 participants were used. The 200 participants were either given a directed consultation that included statements such as 'You are suffering from …', and 'It is essential that you take this medication'; 'You should be better in _____ days' and 'Come and see me in _____ days', or they received a sharing consultation that included statements such as 'What do you think is wrong?' and 'Would you like a prescription?'; 'Are there any other problems?' and 'When would you like to come and see me again?'. The consultations were tape-recorded. The patients were given two questionnaires, one immediately after the consultation and one a week later, to assess their satisfaction with the consultation.

Results: Overall the patients reported a high level of satisfaction with their consultations. However, the group who had received the directed consultation reported a higher level of satisfaction than those in the sharing group. The directed group reported significantly higher levels of satisfaction with the explanation given by the doctor, and with their own understanding of the problem, and were more likely to report that they had been 'greatly helped' than the sharing group.

Conclusions: The results show that the style of consultation does affect patient satisfaction, and appears to contradict contemporary conventional ideas that sharing decisions about treatment is popular with patients and enhances the relationship between doctor and patient.

Increasingly doctors are trained in interpersonal skills in medical school and are taught skills such as **active listening**. Active listening can help the patient to communicate more easily. It includes using eye contact, open-ended questions and responding positively to patients, while listening to their descriptions of their problems. These kinds of skill are taught through role-play and observation with real patients. There is evidence that this kind of training does improve communication skills (Weinman, 1997).

Initially, student doctors may face many problems when trying to interview patients. In a study of interviewing techniques, Batenburg and Gerritsma (1983) note that, in particular, students report how hard it can be to initiate conversation in the consultation, decide on the range of possible diagnoses and cope with the emotions of their patients.

Maguire and Rutter (1976) argue that a useful strategy for medical students is to use video to see themselves interacting with patients. In one study students were divided into two groups – one in which they used video during a consultation with a patient, and a control group in which they did not have access to this feedback. The video group were also given written notes of a model for interviewing recommended by Maguire. A week later the medical students in both groups interviewed a second patient. The experimental condition gained three times as much relevant information from the patients as the control condition.

In their model of an appropriate interviewing technique, Maguire and Rutter distinguish between the **content** of the interview (that is, what information is collected) and the **process** (how it is collected):

- The **content** of the interview should contain the following:

  - Details of the problem: the doctor should recognize that there may be more than one problem and that these could be emotional and social, as well as physical. Having established the main cause of concern, the doctor should ask if there are any other problems the patient might like to mention.
  - Impact on patient and his or her family: the doctor should find out about the effect of the illness on the patient's relationships with family members, work, and his or her emotional state.
  - Patients' view of their problems: patients' beliefs about their illnesses are very important as they can often explain the patients' behaviour in relation to their illness. If the doctor understands patients' views, he or she can help them by providing reassurance and explaining the importance of treatment, for example.
  - Predisposition to develop similar problems: the patient's background and early health record may be important.
  - Screening questions: these questions should provide the opportunity for the doctor to touch on areas that have not been covered. If, for example, the doctor has concentrated on the patient's physical well-being then he or she might ask about that patient's psychological state.

- The **process** should include the following.

  - Beginning the interview: the doctor should greet patients appropriately and show them where to sit if they have not met before, in order to put them at their ease.
  - The procedure of the interview: to help patients understand what is happening, the doctor should explain how the interview will take place in order to put patients at their ease. For example, the doctor should explain if he or she is going to take notes.
  - Obtaining relevant information: doctors frequently interrupt their patients, but it is better for doctors to ask open-ended questions, then

encourage a response from the patient by using active listening techniques.

– Ending the interview: it is important to allow time at the end of a consultation to allow the patient to ask questions and for the doctor to review and sum up what has been discussed.

One of the most difficult areas of communication relates to breaking bad news. Trainee doctors are now taught how best to convey this kind of information and how to deal with distressed patients or relatives. What is appropriate for one person may be difficult for another to cope with. Non-verbal behaviour may give clues as to how the patient feels – whether he or she is embarrassed, for example.

Hogbin and Fallowfield (1989) describe a simple procedure that can help to communicate difficult or sensitive information concerning certain types of diagnosis. They recommend using a tape-recording of the consultation, which the patient can then take away. This helps patients and relatives to go back to information that they may have found too overwhelming to grasp at the time of the consultation.

Another good example of a situation in which effective communication is very important is before stressful medical procedures or investigations. Written information can be helpful in this context, since the patient can refer to it and understand it in advance of the procedure. There is evidence that clear information about the procedure can help patients cope much better with what they are about to face as RLA 7 shows.

Real Life Application 7:

Brain scan information leaflet

Patients who are about to undergo a brain scan are given a simple leaflet that has a list of information points about the process involved. The leaflet provides information about the scanner and about what happens after the scan:

- Magnetic Resonance Imaging and Spectroscopy is explained.
- The patient is reassured that no X-rays are used.
- The patient is told that he or she will not see or feel anything, but will hear a knocking noise during the procedure.
- The patient is informed that the procedure will take about one hour.
- The patient is informed that the scanner is open at both ends.

- The patient is asked to remain still during the procedure.
- The leaflet explains that the scanner is light and ventilated, and that there is a two-way intercom if the patient needs to communicate with the hospital staff at any time.
- The patient is told that if he or she wears contact lenses, the lenses may have to be removed.
- The patient is given a telephone number that he or she can call if there are any questions.
- The leaflet explains that the results will be sent back to the patient's consultant after a week to ten days.

Adaptation of an advice leaflet given to brain scan patients at Addenbrookes Hospital, Cambridge.

Summary

- Information is provided for the patient in a simple and straightforward list form, explaining what the patient can expect during the scanning procedure.

Questions

1 Why do hospitals produce information leaflets of the type explained in RLA 7?

2 What do you think is the most important information contained in the description of the list in RLA 7? Why?

Payne and Walker (1996) are interested in how doctors engage in what Goffman (1971) calls **impression management**. They argue that learning to become a doctor involves more than just knowledge, claiming that being a doctor also includes looking and behaving like a doctor. It involves a hierarchical relationship with nursing staff and patients, in which it is clear who is in charge. They argue that doctors have their own particular 'props' that set them apart from other people in the hospital and define who they are – the stethoscope and the white coat, for example. This role management is used by some doctors more than others – for example, doctors who work in out-patient clinics are starting to adopt a more informal style.

Practitioner communication and style

As discussed in the previous section, doctors have different styles in the way they deal with patients. These were described as:

- doctor-centred
- co-operative
- patient-centred.

Doctor-centred relationships

These are characterized by the doctor taking charge of the interaction. There have been a number of studies carried out into the interaction between doctors and their patients, and these appear to confirm that the majority of interactions are still based on a doctor-centred style. These studies categorize interaction into groups of behaviours. In a meta-analysis of some of these studies, Roter (1989) found that doctors:

- give information in approximately 35% of their communications
- ask for information in about 22% of their communications
- talk positively to the patient about 15% of the time and negatively about 1% of the time
- try to relate to their patients 10% of the time (what Roter calls 'partnership building') and make social conversation 6% of the time

However, patients give information about 50% of the time, and ask questions less than 10% of the time.

Patient-centred relationships

These are characterized by more open-ended questions and allow more time for patients to raise their own concerns. It is often possible to tell the style of the doctor by the length of the waiting time in his or her surgery. Patients often choose which of the doctors to visit at the local practice depending on the nature of their problem. If it is a straightforward medical problem that they already understand and for which they may simply need some penicillin, the patient may choose one doctor. If their problem is less specific or they need some support and advice

Patient-centred responses	Doctor-centred responses
Open questions	Closed questions
Listening	Direct questions
Reflecting	Reassurance
Clarifying	Giving advice
Indications of understanding and acceptance	
	Kent and Dalgleish, 1996.

Figure 3.1: Patient-centred and doctor-centred responses

from their doctor, the person may choose a different member of the practice. An example of the main differences between these two approaches is summarized in the Figure 3.1.

Although these styles have been described as quite different, one is not necessarily better or worse than the other. Individual patients prefer different styles and if they have a choice, such as that within General Practice, they will chose to consult with the doctor who suits their own style best.

Key Study 6 illustrates the style of communication that health professionals in a hospital setting often use and offers suggestions for their motivation in doing this.

KEY STUDY 6

Researchers: Bourhis, Roth and MacQueen (1989)

Aim: Bourhis *et al* were interested in finding out what factors affect communication between hospital staff and their patients. Their aims were to examine the relationship between:

a the use of language between health professionals and their patients

b the motivation either to change or to maintain the type of language used

c the norms of communication in a hospital, and

d the status and power differences that categorize patients, doctors and nurses.

Method: The study was carried out using three groups of respondents: 40 doctors, 40 student nurses and 40 patients. All respondents were asked to complete a written questionnaire about the use of medical language (ML) and everyday language (EL) in the hospital setting. The questionnaire consisted of 4 sections. The first section asked about the amount of medical and everyday language the respondent used in the hospital with members of the other groups in the study. The second section

---

asked the respondent to estimate how much ML and EL other members of their own group used with the other groups in the study. The third section asked the respondent to evaluate (on a 7-point scale) the appropriateness of the use of ML and EL among the study groups in the hospital setting. The fourth section asked the respondents for background information and about their attitudes to various communication issues in the hospital.

Results: Doctors' self-reports of their efforts to use EL with their patients was confirmed by other doctors but not by patients or nurses. Patients self-reports stated that they themselves used EL, although those with limited knowledge of ML used this to try to communicate better with doctors. Doctors, however, did not encourage the use of ML by their patients, and reported the strongest preference of all the groups for patients to use EL. Nurses were reported to have a very particular role by all three groups in their use of both EL and ML. They were seen as 'communication brokers' between the EL of the patient group and the ML of the group of doctors. The nurses were perceived as being able to mediate between the doctors and their patients. All three groups agreed that EL was better for use with patients, and that use of ML often led to difficulties in communication.

Conclusions: One of the overall conclusions drawn from the results of the study was that doctors used ML as a way of maintaining their status in relation to their patient group. Their use of ML was also interpreted as a way of maintaining the power and prestige accorded to doctors within society as a whole. Therefore there is a strong

motivation for them to maintain (or even increase) their use of ML. The fact that nurses were prepared to 'converge' with the doctors and patients is taken as an indication that they are less status conscious than doctors, as they are trained to know ML, just as doctors are. Bourhis *et al* suggest that the results show that experienced doctors and nurses, as well as students, might benefit from courses focused on effective communication between hospital staff and patients. They also note that a better understanding of the motivation behind the use of language may help to avoid communication breakdown between health workers and their patients.

Patient communication and style

Like doctors, patients have different ways of communicating that can either help or hinder the doctor. For example, patients with the same condition may well focus on very different symptoms, and describe these to the doctor. The doctor has to be very aware of the possibility of this happening. Some patients who go to see a doctor about a specific medical problem might actually have other problems they want to discuss with the doctor. Although the doctor needs to allow for the possibility of a range of problems presenting themselves, it can make it more difficult for the doctor to find the root cause of the problem. On the other hand, patients might find it difficult to express their symptoms clearly, and this again might make it possible for the doctor to misinterpret or misdiagnose.

A further consideration is that patients might also find it difficult to speak to the doctor for social or cultural reasons. It may be inappropriate for an Asian woman to see a male doctor, or if she does she may not feel at ease explaining symptoms. While this is obviously not the fault of the patient it can make it difficult to communicate effectively. Language barriers and cultural differences can sometimes be a problem, too.

Non-verbal communication

As well as the obvious need for verbal communication, a great deal of the interaction between doctor and patient takes place at a non-verbal level. Non-verbal communication can influence verbal communication to a considerable degree. Whether patients perceive their doctor to be receptive and understanding may relate to the non-verbal signals he or she is giving, just as much, if not more, than the verbal ones. Similarly, the response of patients will tell the doctor a certain amount about how they are feeling, how receptive they are to what the doctor may be saying, and how likely they are to be able to adhere to the treatments and instructions that have been given.

Facial expressions, as well as other forms of body language, can be closely related to a person's emotional state and can indicate to the doctor how the patient is feeling. Eye contact tells the patient and the doctor whether the other person is listening. It is usual to maintain a degree of eye contact when listening to another person. Eye contact can be used by a doctor to gauge whether patients understand what is being said, whereas patients might look at the eye contact a doctor is making in order to gauge his or her interest in and empathy with them.

Figure 3.2 shows three ways a person could enter a consulting room.

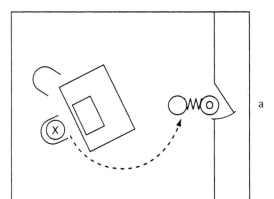

a Here, person 'O' steps into the office, while person 'X' rises to greet him or her; 'O' is considered to have higher status than 'X'.

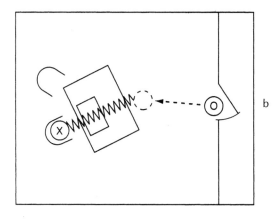

b Here, 'O' moves towards 'X', who remains seated; 'O' is seen as having lower status than 'X'.

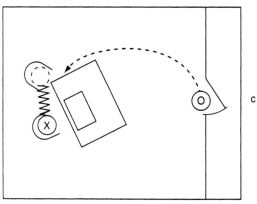

c One situation in which both 'O' and 'X' are considered to be of equal status; 'O' moves towards 'X' and sits beside him or her without hesitation.

Burns, 1964.
Reproduced with permission from *New Scientist Magazine*,
www.newscientist.com

Figure 3.2: Impacts of furniture positioning in consulting rooms

Videotaped research suggests that patients talk while the doctor makes eye contact, and hesitate or stop talking when the doctor looks away or starts making notes.

Posture and position in the consulting room can facilitate or hinder a consultation. Leaning towards the patient can be interpreted as the doctor showing interest in that patient. Restlessness on the part of the doctor or the patient can be interpreted in different ways – as perhaps the desire to end the consultation if it is the doctor who is being restless, and as a need to change the subject or to say something else on the part of the patient. The doctor must be particularly aware of these cues, so that they understand how to help the patient say what they want to communicate to the doctor, without feeling intimidated or uncomfortable in the presence of the doctor.

The position of the doctor, but also of his or her desk, is important. Status can be related to the position of the desk in a consultation room, and to the position of the doctor behind the desk. An example of the importance of the position of the furniture in a consulting room is shown in Figure 3.2 (see page 59).

Commentary

- Effective communication between doctor and patient is fundamental in situations where patients are expected to make important decisions affecting their own or a relative's health.
- Effective communication can reduce patient anxiety about procedures and treatments.
- Without effective communication patients can become unsure or unhappy about their treatments, which may lead to non-adherence or mistrust of the doctor.

Essay questions

1 Describe and evaluate factors that contribute to people's non-adherence to medical advice.

2 Describe and evaluate what psychologists have discovered about patient–practitioner relationships.

3 Describe and evaluate ways in which adherence to medical advice can be improved.

4 Specific health psychology issues

This chapter looks at the specific health-related issues of pain and stress. It examines these conditions in detail, and focuses on measuring, managing and controlling these conditions. The chapter also looks at examples of chronic and terminal illnesses, and focuses on psychological factors affecting people with these illnesses. Real Life Applications that are considered are:

- RLA 8: Congenital analgesia
- RLA 9: Managing anxiety

Pain

Everybody experiences pain at one time or another in their lives, and the most obvious association for most people is between pain and injury – the more severe the injury the worse the pain. However, it is not uncommon for people who have been severely injured not to feel pain (at least for a certain period of time) and for people who are not injured, or who have recovered from an injury, to experience lasting pain. These are examples of a number of phenomena that are difficult to explain and that have lead many of those who write about pain to describe what they call the 'puzzle' of pain (Melzack and Wall, 1996). Some of the most interesting examples of the problematic relationship between injury and pain come from societies where 'painful' ceremonies accompany some stages of initiation, or have ritual or religious significance. In some cases tissue damage can be quite severe and yet the 'sufferer' shows no signs of pain. Pain is obviously multidimensional in its nature – do these people experience no pain because of heightened state of arousal? Or is it inappropriate to show pain?

It is very important to try to understand pain: according to Karoly it is:

[the] *most pervasive symptom in medical practice, the most frequently stated 'cause' of disability, and the single most compelling force underlying an individual's choice to seek or avoid medical care (1985, p. 461).*

Pain can dominate the lives of those who suffer from it, and it can affect work and social relationships.

What is pain?

One of the most difficult problems all those who try to understand pain have is simply trying to define it. One of the difficulties in discussing pain is that there is still no adequate definition, not least because of the diversity of pain experienced by different individuals. Melzack and Wall say:

The word 'pain' represents a category of experiences, signifying a multitude of different, unique experiences having different causes, and characterized by different qualities varying along a number of sensory, affective and evaluative dimensions (1996, p. 46).

Some of the more simplistic definitions look at pain from a physiological perspective; others have tried to incorporate the emotional component of pain. For example, Merskey (1986) define pain as 'an unpleasant sensory and emotional experience associated with actual or potential tissue damage, or described in terms of such damage'.

The purpose of pain

For most people pain can serve a number of useful functions:

- **Prevention of further injury**: pain caused by damage or injury can prevent a more severe injury from occurring, such as the warning pain from a blister on your foot telling you not to carry on walking.
- **Learning**: the pain caused by a burn would teach a child to avoid touching a hot stove.

- **Aiding recovery:** an ankle that has been sprained hurts to make the injured person rest the limb so that the injury can heal.
- **Warning:** pain can warn the individual of an underlying illness and encourage him or her to seek medical attention.

However, many people suffer from pain that appears to serve no useful purpose and this is more difficult to explain. A good example of this is **phantom limb pain**, where a limb may cause excruciating pain long after it has been amputated. A very high proportion of people who have had amputations suffer from phantom limb pain. Jensen *et al* (1983) found that 65% of amputees suffered pain in a phantom limb six months after the amputation. This pain was still felt by 60% after two years. Pain in phantom limbs can be severe and is described by sufferers as 'cramping, shooting, burning or crushing'. There is no single factor explanation of phantom limb pain. There is obviously a link to the nervous system and activity in the spinal cord and in the brain, but none of the connections that have been made can explain all the phenomena associated with phantom limb pain.

Rather than providing any of the functions listed above, pain such as this can become the overwhelming problem in itself. Pain such as this can cause people to become very depressed and can affect much more than their physical well-being. Their work is likely to be affected and relationships with family members, for example, may suffer. Another example of such pain is known as **trigeminal neuralgia**, where slight pressure on certain parts of the face or mouth can cause extremely severe pain.

Types and theories of pain

Pain is not just a simple sensation; it can vary in quality, intensity, duration, location and frequency. Pain can be 'sharp' or 'throbbing', constant or intermittent. The type of pain a person experiences will differ according to the origin and duration of the pain. In describing different types of pain, people often refer to the distinction between **organic** and **psychogenic** pain:

- **Organic pain** is that which is obviously related to tissue damage and when the pain is largely caused by that damage.
- **Psychogenic pain** is where the underlying causes are seen to be largely psychological.

Most contemporary researchers recognize, in fact, that there is a close link between the two, and that organic and psychogenic factors play an important role in the experience of most pain. The absence of an obvious cause does not imply that the pain is not real and this is important to recognize. A study by Gillmore and Hill (1981) showed that nursing students were seen to react less favourably to the pain of patients who did not have a specific diagnosis – in other words, they valued a medical diagnosis more than the patients' subjective experience.

There are a number of different terms commonly used in the literature and language to describe pain.

Acute and chronic pain

One of the distinctions that is made it between accute and chronic pain:

- **Acute pain** is an intense pain that lasts until healing has begun – for example, the pain of appendicitis or of a broken limb.
- **Chronic pain** is much more persistent. It can be constant or intermittent and pain is said to be chronic if it has lasted for three months or more.

Rigge (1990) carried out a survey on approximately 1000 people and found that 7% of the population in the UK has been in pain for three months or more. The prevalence of chronic pain increases with age: from 15–24 years, 4% of people suffer chronic pain; between 25 and 34, 5% suffer chronic pain; between 35 and 44, the figure rises to 7%; between 45 and 54, it rises to 10%; and over 55 years of age it is 20% and increasing (Bowsher, 1993).

Acute pain describes temporary pain that is distressing, but the worry will reduce as the condition improves. This type of pain is often the consequence of injury or trauma, or of an acute inflammatory illness. Chronic pain often increases or maintains high levels of anxiety. When medical treatment has not helped, the pain can take over the lives of those who suffer from it, and people with chronic pain can develop a desperate sense of helplessness and hopelessness.

Referred pain

External pain is easy to locate at the point of injury, but internal pain is often 'referred' from the actual site of the problem. **Referred pain** can be acute or chronic. A well-known example of referred pain is caused by appendicitis. The first sign of appendicitis is often pain in the middle of the upper abdomen, while the appendix itself is on the lower right-hand side of the abdomen. With angina and heart attacks, severe pain is often felt in the left arm.

Injury without pain

This may take the form of either **episodic analgesia** or **congenital analgesia**.

- **Episodic analgesia** is a reasonably common condition and, in fact, most of us have experienced this at some time in our lives. It occurs when a person injures him or herself but does not feel the pain for some minutes or hours afterwards. In our everyday lives, we sometimes cut or bruise ourselves and do not notice the pain until later. Much of the research that has been carried out on the occurrence of episodic analgesia has focused on the victims of traumatic injury through war. Beecher (1959) conducted a study on the behaviour of soldiers who had severe abdominal injuries inflicted during battle in the Second World War. Two-thirds of those he observed denied having any pain or reported so little pain that they did not need medication.

Carlen *et al* (1979) carried out a similar study of Israeli soldiers who lost limbs in the Yom Kippur War. They did not feel any pain from these injuries until many hours after they had been wounded. Carlen argues that they were fully aware of the situation and were surprised that they felt no pain.

However, not all research on episodic analgesia is carried out on victims of war. Melzack *et al* (1982) carried out a study on accident victims who arrived at the emergency room of a city hospital and found that they did not feel pain for minutes or hours after the injury. In these cases episodic analgesia must be either an accidental or an adaptive reaction to the situation, which causes a withdrawal from the pain even if, as Carlen suggests, the victim is not in shock.

- **Congenital analgesia** is a very rare condition in which some people are born without the ability to feel pain at all. These cases are well documented and have generated a great deal of research. This condition is illustrated in RLA 8.

Real Life Application 8:
Congenital analgesia

A well-known case of congenital insensitivity to pain is a girl referred to as 'Miss C' who was a student at McGill University in Montreal in the 1950s. She was normal in every way, except that she could not feel pain. When she was a child she had bitten off the tip of her tongue and had suffered third-degree burns by kneeling on a radiator. When she was examined by a psychologist (Charles Murray) in 1950 she did not feel any pain when she was given strong electric shocks or when exposed to very hot and very cold water. When these stimuli were presented to her she showed no change in heart rate, blood pressure or respiration. She did not remember ever having coughed or sneezed, and did not show a blinking reflex. She died at the age of 29 as a result of her condition.

Although during a post-mortem there were no obvious signs of what had caused the analgesia in the first place, she had damaged her knees, hips and spine. This damage was due to the fact that she did not shift her weight when standing or sitting, did not turn over in bed and did not avoid what would normally be considered to be uncomfortable postures. This caused severe inflammation in her joints.

Although there is some evidence that this condition may be inherited, there are other causes such as neurological damage. However, some cases cannot be explained in this way. Most

During a match or competition, sportspeople injure themselves but most appear to feel no pain, preferring to carry on with the game they are playing. Their injuries are often serious enough to require at least some medical attention later.

people with this condition learn to avoid causing themselves too much harm but, as in the case of 'Miss C', may die as a result of the problems caused by the analgesia.

Adapted from Melzack and Wall, 1996.

Summary

- Congenital analgesia is a very rare condition that is more serious and less well understood than episodic analgesia.
- It stops sufferers feeling any sensation of pain.
- It may be an inherited condition, or it may be caused by neurological damage.

Questions

1 How is congenital analgesia different from episodic analgesia? Give examples.

2 What strategies might a person with this condition have to employ to avoid serious illness and injury?

Pain without injury

There are many people who feel pain for which there is no known cause. Back pain often has no apparent physiological basis, and certain types of headaches such as migraines have no proven pathology, although there are different theories as to what caused them. Two types of pain that are often described as *not* being caused by injury are **causalgia** and **neuralgia**:

- **Causalgia** is described as severe, burning pain; it appears to occur at the location of some previous severe injury and is caused by nerve damage. Only a minority of patients with such wounds develop causalgia, but the pain lasts for a long time after the wound has completely healed. The pain can occur straightaway after injury or be delayed for months. The skin can become very sensitive to touch, radiating out from the original location of the wound.
- **Neuralgia** occurs in various forms and like causalgia it is associated with peripheral nerve damage. However, neuralgia is a different type of pain to causalgia. Neuralgic pain is described as shooting or stabbing along the pathway of a nerve. Neuralgia can occur suddenly and commonly as the result of very gentle stimulation. Trigeminal neuralgia (mentioned on page 62) is a particularly unpleasant form of neuralgia that can be very debilitating and make it difficult for a person to eat properly, since crisp hard food might cause intense stabbing pain.

Phantom limb pain

The experience of a person feeling a 'phantom' limb when he or she has had a limb amputated is common. However, some people can experience severe pain in these phantoms long after they have been amputated. Jensen's study (mentioned on page 62) found that 65% of patients experienced pain in their phantom limbs. As with other pain that occurs without a physical basis, phantom limb pain is perhaps associated with neural damage, although as was discussed earlier the phantom limb pain appears to be more complex than this.

Early pain theories

Early pain theories describe pain within a biomedical framework. These theories work on the assumption that there is an automatic response to pain. Descartes (who is mentioned in Chapter 1, page 3) was one of the earliest writers on pain. He believed that there was a direct pathway from the source of the pain to an area in the brain that detected painful sensations.

- **Specificity theory:** developed by Von Frey (1895), this theory argues that the body has separate sensory receptors for perceiving touch, heat and pain and that these receptors are sensitive to particular sensations.
- **Pattern theory:** this is based on similar assumptions of the relationship between the stimulus and the response. Pattern theory, however, argues that there is no separate system for perceiving pain and that the receptors for pain are shared with other senses such as touch. Pattern theory argues that too much stimulation can cause pain.

Both these theories assume that the sensation of pain has a single cause and that it is tissue damage that causes pain. Neither theory includes a psychological approach to pain, and organic pain is seen as the only 'real' pain.

Gate Control Theory

Melzack and Wall developed the Gate Control Theory in the 1960s to explain types of pain that were recognized but could not be understood in terms of the previous models of pain. Examples of this type of pain include phantom limb pain and tension headaches. The Gate Control Model also explains the lack of pain under certain circumstances, such as episodic analgesia after traumatic injury. Gate Control Theory adds a psychological component to an understanding of pain.

Melzack and Wall (1965) argue that there is a neural 'gate' in the spinal cord. Evidence suggests that this is true, although there is no physical gate that can be identified. Gate Control Theory is a model that operates 'as if' there is a gate that can be opened and closed by different factors (see Figure 4.1). According to gate control theory there are three factors that affect our experience of pain and open and close the gate:

- the amount of activity in the pain fibres
- the amount of activity in other peripheral fibres
- messages that descend from the brain.

The stronger the pain, the more activity there is in the pain fibres, which causes the gate to open. **Counter stimulation** causes activity in the peripheral fibres that carry messages about other more harmless sensations, and this can act to close the gate. This is why 'rubbing it better' really works. Messages from the brain can either open or close the gate. Anxiety about the pain may open the gate, while distraction or relaxation may close that gate (see Table 4.1).

Measuring pain

Pain is a subjective experience and it is impossible to feel or to observe directly other people's pain, so it has to be measured indirectly, by communicating with the sufferer. Also, because pain is multidimensional, a range of questions need to be asked in

	Conditions that open the gate	Conditions that close the gate
Physical	extent of injury; inappropriate activity level	medication; counter stimulation
Emotional	anxiety; depression; tension	positive emotions; relaxation; rest
Mental	focusing on the pain; boredom	distraction; involvement in activities

Table 4.1: Different factors that open and close the 'gate'

order to get information about these different dimensions. Perception of pain is modified by a wide range of situational, behavioural and emotional factors making it an especially subjective experience. This means that other people's pain is very difficult to assess.

The assessment of pain is important for research and as a diagnostic tool for medical treatment. Studies that attempt to discover factors that affect people's perception of pain, or to determine the effectiveness of pain management strategies, need reliable and valid ways of assessing pain. The fact that pain measures tend to be very subjective can cause difficulties for researchers.

There are three commonly used measures of pain:

- physiological measures of pain
- observation of pain behaviours
- self-report techniques.

Physiological measures of pain

The most obvious way to measure pain physiologically is to assess the extent of the tissue damage or injury: that is, the more injured someone is, the more pain they must be in. However, as mentioned above, the relationship between tissue damage and the subjective experience of pain is very complex and this is not a valid way of assessing pain; it is necessary to look for other physiological signs of pain.

Muscle tension is associated with painful conditions such as headaches and lower backache, and it can be measured using an **electromyograph** (EMG). This apparatus measures electrical activity in the muscles, which is a sign of how tense they are. Some link has been established between headaches and EMG patterns, but EMG recordings do not generally correlate with pain perception (Chapman *et al*, 1985) and EMG measurements have not been shown to be a useful way of measuring pain.

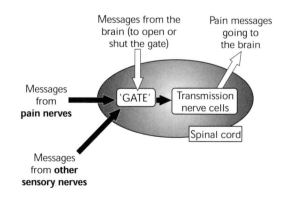

Figure 4.1: The Gate Control Theory

Another approach has been to relate pain to **autonomic arousal**. By taking measures of pulse rate, skin conductance and skin temperature, it may be possible to measure the physiological arousal caused by experiencing pain.

Finally, since pain is perceived within the brain, it may be possible to measure brain activity, using an **electroencephalograph** (EEG), in order to determine the extent to which an individual is experiencing pain. It has been shown that subjective reports of pain do correlate with electrical changes that show up as peaks in EEG recordings. Moreover, when analgesics are given, both pain report and waveform amplitude on the EEG are decreased (Chapman *et al*, 1985).

Commentary

The advantage of the physiological measures of pain described above is that they are objective (that is, not subject to bias by the person whose pain is being measured, or by the person measuring the pain). On the other hand, they involve the use of expensive machinery and trained personnel. Their main disadvantage, however, is that they are not valid (that is, they do not measure what they say they are measuring). For example, autonomic arousal can occur in the absence of pain – being wired up to a machine may be stressful and can cause a person's heart rate to increase. A person's perception of their pain may also affect their level of arousal; whether or not they believe this treatment will work or how serious they perceive their pain to be. In other words, if someone is very anxious about the process of having his or her pain assessed, or else is worried about the meaning of the pain, this will cause physiological changes not necessarily related to the intensity of the pain being experienced.

Observations of pain behaviours

People tend to behave in certain ways when they are in pain; observing such behaviour could provide a means of assessing pain.

Turk, Wack and Kerns (1985) have provided a classification of observable pain behaviours.

- **Facial /audible expression of distress:** grimacing and teeth clenching; moaning and sighing.
- **Distorted ambulation or posture:** limping or walking with a stoop; moving slowly or carefully to protect an injury; supporting, rubbing or holding a painful spot; frequently shifting position.
- **Negative effect**: feeling irritable; asking for help in walking, or to be excused from activities; ask-

ing questions like 'Why did this happen to me?'.
- **Avoidance of activity:** lying down frequently; avoiding physical activity; using a prosthetic device.

These pain behaviours are a way of communicating to other people that we are suffering pain, and therefore can be observed by others.

One way to assess pain behaviours is to observe them in a clinical setting. Keefe and Williams (1992) have identified five elements that need to be considered when preparing to assess any form of behaviour through this type of observation.

- **A rationale for observation:** it is important for clinicians to know why they are observing pain behaviours. One reason is to identify 'problem' behaviours that the patient may be reluctant to report, such as pain when swallowing, so that treatment can be given. Another is to monitor the progress of a course of treatment.
- **A method for sampling pain behaviour:** techniques for sampling and recording behaviour include continuous observation, measuring duration (how long the patient takes to complete a task), frequency counts (the number of times a target behaviour occurs) and time sampling (for example, observing the patient for five minutes every hour).
- **Definitions of the behaviour:** observers need to be completely clear as to what behaviours they are looking for.
- **Observer training:** in most clinical situations, there will be different observers at different times and it is important that they are consistent.
- **Reliability and validity:** the most useful measure of consistency in observation methods is inter-rater reliability, but test-retest reliability can also be useful. Three types of validity that could be assessed are: concurrent validity (are the results of the observation consistent with another measure of the same behaviour?), construct validity (are the behaviours being recorded really signs of pain?) and discriminant validity (do the observation records discriminate between patients with and without pain?).

A commonly used example of an observation tool for assessing pain behaviour is the **UAB Pain Behaviour Scale** designed by Richards *et al* (1982). This scale consists of ten target behaviours and observers have to rate how frequently each occurs (see Figure 4.2). The UAB is easy to use and quick

UAB PAIN BEHAVIOUR SCALE

Name: . . . .

Rater: . . . .

	Date:	M	T	W	T	F	S	S	M	T	W	T	F	S	S	M	T	W	T	F	S	S
1 Vocal complaints: verbal	None	1	1	1	1	1	1	1	1	1	1	1	1	1	1	1	1	1	1	1	1	1
	Occasional	½	½	½	½	½	½	½	½	½	½	½	½	½	½	½	½	½	½	½	½	½
	Frequent	0	0	0	0	0	0	0	0	0	0	0	0	0	0	0	0	0	0	0	0	0
2 Vocal complaints: non-verbal *(moans, groans, gasps, etc)*	None	1	1	1	1	1	1	1	1	1	1	1	1	1	1	1	1	1	1	1	1	1
	Occasional	½	½	½	½	½	½	½	½	½	½	½	½	½	½	½	½	½	½	½	½	½
	Frequent	0	0	0	0	0	0	0	0	0	0	0	0	0	0	0	0	0	0	0	0	0
3 Down-time *(time spent lying down per day because of pain: 8 am–8 pm)*	None	1	1	1	1	1	1	1	1	1	1	1	1	1	1	1	1	1	1	1	1	1
	0–60 min	½	½	½	½	½	½	½	½	½	½	½	½	½	½	½	½	½	½	½	½	½
	>60 min	0	0	0	0	0	0	0	0	0	0	0	0	0	0	0	0	0	0	0	0	0
4 Facial grimaces	None	1	1	1	1	1	1	1	1	1	1	1	1	1	1	1	1	1	1	1	1	1
	Mild and/or infrequent	½	½	½	½	½	½	½	½	½	½	½	½	½	½	½	½	½	½	½	½	½
	Severe and/or infrequent	0	0	0	0	0	0	0	0	0	0	0	0	0	0	0	0	0	0	0	0	0
5 Standing posture	Normal	1	1	1	1	1	1	1	1	1	1	1	1	1	1	1	1	1	1	1	1	1
	Mildly impaired	½	½	½	½	½	½	½	½	½	½	½	½	½	½	½	½	½	½	½	½	½
	Distorted	0	0	0	0	0	0	0	0	0	0	0	0	0	0	0	0	0	0	0	0	0
6 Mobility	No visible impairment	1	1	1	1	1	1	1	1	1	1	1	1	1	1	1	1	1	1	1	1	1
	Mild limp and/or laboured walking	½	½	½	½	½	½	½	½	½	½	½	½	½	½	½	½	½	½	½	½	½
	Marked limp and/or laboured walking	0	0	0	0	0	0	0	0	0	0	0	0	0	0	0	0	0	0	0	0	0
7 Body language *(clutching, rubbing site of pain)*	None	1	1	1	1	1	1	1	1	1	1	1	1	1	1	1	1	1	1	1	1	1
	Occasional	½	½	½	½	½	½	½	½	½	½	½	½	½	½	½	½	½	½	½	½	½
	Frequent	0	0	0	0	0	0	0	0	0	0	0	0	0	0	0	0	0	0	0	0	0
8 Use of visible supportive equipment *(braces, crutches, cane, leaning on furniture, TENS, etc). Do not score if equipment prescribed*	None	1	1	1	1	1	1	1	1	1	1	1	1	1	1	1	1	1	1	1	1	1
	Occasional	½	½	½	½	½	½	½	½	½	½	½	½	½	½	½	½	½	½	½	½	½
	Dependent: constant use	0	0	0	0	0	0	0	0	0	0	0	0	0	0	0	0	0	0	0	0	0
9 Stationary movement	Sits or stands still	1	1	1	1	1	1	1	1	1	1	1	1	1	1	1	1	1	1	1	1	1
	Occasional shifts of position	½	½	½	½	½	½	½	½	½	½	½	½	½	½	½	½	½	½	½	½	½
	Constant movement, position shifts	0	0	0	0	0	0	0	0	0	0	0	0	0	0	0	0	0	0	0	0	0
10 Medication	None	1	1	1	1	1	1	1	1	1	1	1	1	1	1	1	1	1	1	1	1	1
	Non-narcotic analgesic and/or pychogenic medications as prescribed	½	½	½	½	½	½	½	½	½	½	½	½	½	½	½	½	½	½	½	½	½
	Demands for increased dosage or frequency, and/or narcotics, and/or medication abuse	0	0	0	0	0	0	0	0	0	0	0	0	0	0	0	0	0	0	0	0	0
	TOTAL																					

Figure 4.2: The UAB Pain Behaviour Scale

to score; it has scored well on inter-rater and test-retest reliability.

However, correlation between scores on the UAB and on the McGill Pain Questionnaire (see Figure 4.3, page 69) is low indicating that the relationship between observable pain behaviour and the self-reports of the subjective experience of pain is not a close one. This is perhaps not surprising given the number of social and psychological factors that can affect what people say about their pain (for example, anxiety, depression, the need to let others know how ill they are and so on).

Turk *et al* (1983) describe techniques that someone living with the patient (the observer) can use to provide a record of their pain behaviour. These include asking the observer to keep a pain diary, which includes a record of when the patient is in pain and for how long, how the observer recognized the pain, what the observer thought and felt at the time, and how the observer attempted to help the patient alleviate the pain. Other techniques are to interview the observer, or to ask the observer to complete a questionnaire containing questions about how much the pain interferes with the patient's normal activities and social life, the effect of the pain on family relationships and on the moods of both patient and observer.

Commentary

- Behavioural assessment is less objective than taking physiological measurements, because it relies on the observer's interpretation of the patient's pain behaviours (although, in practice, this can be partly dealt with by using clearly defined checklists of behaviour and carrying out inter-rater reliability – that is, using two independent observers and comparing their findings).

- Because pain behaviours are controllable by the individual and, unlike the actual experience of pain itself, are observable by others, they may be susceptible to reinforcement. The fact that pain behaviour can be affected by social reinforcement weakens the link between observable behaviour and the experience of pain. In other words, an individual may be displaying a great deal of pain behaviour, not because that individual is in severe pain but because he or she is receiving social reinforcement for the pain behaviour (for example, attention, sympathy and time off work). The study by Gil *et al* (1988, see Chapter 1, page 8) provides an example of this: the children whose pain behaviour (scratching their eczema) was rewarded with attention exhibited more of this behaviour.

Self-report measures

Because pain is a subjective, internal experience, the assessment of pain is therefore best carried out by using patient self-reports, and this is by far the most frequently used technique.

Carroll (1993a) lists the different dimensions of pain that sufferers can be questioned about:

- **Site of pain:** where is the pain?
- **Type of pain:** what does the pain feel like?
- **Frequency of pain:** how often does the pain occur?
- **Aggravating or relieving factors:** what makes the pain better or worse?
- **Disability:** how does the pain affect the patient's everyday life?
- **Duration of pain:** how long has the pain been present?
- **Response to current and previous treatments:** how effective have drugs and other treatments been?

An important item to add to this list is the emotional and cognitive effect of the pain – in other words, how does the pain make patients feel and how does it affect their thought processes and attitudes?

The McGill Pain Questionnaire

The McGill Pain Questionnaire, developed by Melzack (1975), was the first proper self-report pain measuring instrument and is still the most widely used today.

An attempt to find words to describe experiences of pain was made in a study by Melzack and Torgerson (1971) in which they asked doctors and university graduates to classify 102 adjectives into groups describing different aspects of pain. As a result of this exercise, they identified three major psychological dimensions of pain:

- **sensory:** what the pain feels like physically – where it is located, how intense it is, its duration and its quality (for example, 'burning', 'throbbing')
- **affective:** what the pain feels like emotionally – whether it is frightening, worrying and so on
- **evaluative:** what the subjective overall intensity of the pain experience is (for example, 'unbearable', 'distressing').

Each of the three main classes was divided into a number of sub-classes (sixteen in total). For example, the affective class was sub-divided into tension (including the adjectives 'tiring', 'exhausting'), autonomic (including 'sickening', 'suffocating') and fear (including 'fearful', 'frightful', 'terrifying').

Melzack and Torgerson (1971) then asked a sample of doctors, patients and students to rate the words in each sub-class for intensity. The first 20 questions on the McGill Pain Questionnaire consist of adjectives set out within their sub-classes, in order of intensity. Questions 1 to 10 are sensory, 11 to 15 affective, 16 is evaluative and 17 to 20 are miscellaneous.

Patients are asked to tick the word in each sub-class that best describes their pain. Based on this, a **pain rating index** (PRI) is calculated: each sub-class is effectively a verbal rating scale and is scored

accordingly (that is, 1 for the adjective describing least intensity, 2 for the next one and so on). Scores are given for the different classes (sensory, affective, evaluative and miscellaneous), and also a total score for all the sub-classes. In addition, patients are asked to indicate the location of the pain on a body chart (using the codes E for pain on the surface of the body, I for internal pain and EI for both external and internal), and to indicate present pain intensity (PPI) on a 6-point verbal rating scale. Finally, patients complete a set of three verbal rating scales describing the pattern of the pain. A copy of the McGill Pain Questionnaire can be seen in Figure 4.3.

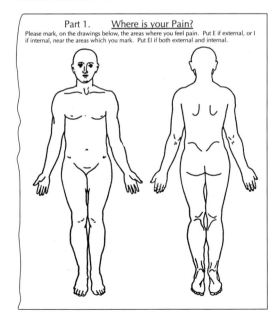

Figure 4.3: Section from McGill pain questionnaire

Commentary

- Although the least objective of the techniques described above, the McGill Pain Questionnaire is considered to be one of the best ways of measuring pain, as it allows the patient to rate his or her own pain in different ways. The fact that there is evidence that people with the same kind of medical condition (for example, toothache or arthritis) tend to be very consistent in their scores on the McGill Pain Questionnaire supports its validity.

- However, quite a wide vocabulary is required in order to complete it; some of the adjectives used in the questionnaire (for example, 'lancinating', 'smarting') have meanings that may not be clear to everyone and may be difficult for the clinician to explain to all patients. Furthermore, the differences in the meanings of some of the words used are very subtle and difficult to understand. As a result, it may not be possible to use the McGill Pain Questionnaire with people whose use of English is limited and it would be difficult to use the McGill Pain Questionnaire with children (see the following section).

Measuring pain in children

An interesting problem with measuring pain is how to do this with children. It seems that even very young children experience pain in much the same way as adults, but the fact that they have limited or no language abilities creates difficulties in assessing their pain. As children mature, they experience an increasingly wide range of physical sensations and learn to describe the various dimensions of the experience of pain in language that is used by those around them – family, friends, what appears on TV.

When questioning young children about their pain, it is important to use vocabulary they are familiar with and to take into account the developmental stage they are at. A three year old would be unable to complete the McGill Pain Questionnaire not only because of the sophisticated vocabulary, but also because the child may not have learnt, for example, to distinguish between internal and external pain.

Observing pain behaviours is a valuable way of measuring pain in children, particularly if they are too young to communicate through the use of language. Such pain behaviours include crying and moaning, flailing about and grimacing (although these behaviours are also carried out in the absence of pain).

Specific scales have been developed for recording pain behaviour in infants, both by parents and health care professionals in a clinical setting. However, the use of pain behaviour scales needs to be treated with caution; behavioural ratings do not always relate exactly to experienced pain intensity. Children can exhibit distress for emotional reasons, even when they are not in pain; some children can be very stoical and calm even though they are suffering. It is important to know the child well when interpreting his or her pain behaviours as signs of suffering.

Because of these difficulties, most ways of assessing pain in children consist of interviews or behavioural assessments, but researchers are now developing appropriate self-report methods. It is possible to ask children about the pain they are experiencing once they have reached a certain age, but certain specific skills are required. It is very important to establish a good rapport with the child and this may be especially difficult if he or she is suffering. Questions have to be asked in the right way, using terminology and concepts that the child is familiar with, and the interviewer has to ensure that the child does indeed understand the questions being asked. Difficult or upsetting questions should be interspersed with easier ones. Finally, the answers given by the children need to be interpreted correctly.

An increasing number of self-report scales for use with children are being developed. Children are able to report how much and what kinds of pain they are experiencing, but the scales used must be appropriate to their developmental level and their language abilities. For example, instead of asking young children to rate intensity of pain on a scale from 1 to 10, they can be presented with a set of line drawings of faces displaying increasingly severe expressions of pain.

The **Varni/Thompson Pediatric Pain Questionnaire** is an example of a self-report scale specifically designed for children (McGrath and Brigham, 1992). This includes visual analogue scales, colour-coded rating scales (in which the children have to pick colours that represent 'no hurt', 'a little hurt', 'more hurt' and 'a lot of hurt', then colour in a body chart) and verbal descriptors to provide information about the sensory, affective and evaluative dimensions of the pain. The questionnaire also asks parents and doctors for information about the child and the family's pain history (including pain relief interventions) and about socioenvironmental factors that might affect the pain.

Controlling pain

Pain management is an area of research that has grown considerably in the last 20 years. Carroll (1993b) argues that this has lead to considerable change in the clinical practice of pain treatment. It is still very common for pain relieving drugs to be the main focus of treatment, especially with acute pain, although drugs are also often used for chronic pain without proper pain assessment. There are obvious reasons for this, when time and money are in short supply, and patients often have a long wait to be referred to a specialist who might use other methods to control and manage their pain.

Attitudes to pain have changed and the idea that pain is to be 'expected' or is 'natural' is outdated. It is now considered that 'patients have a right to no pain' Carroll (1993a, p. 1). Pain relief in childbirth is a good example of this, where **epidural blocks** are widely used in contemporary maternity units. Some of the methods for controlling and managing both acute and chronic pain are considered below.

Medication

The most common form of treatment for both acute and chronic pain is medication of some kind. Doctors choose a drug and a dosage by considering many different factors including the intensity and location of the pain. Interestingly, children are given pain-killing drugs less frequently by doctors than adults, and medical staff stop treating the pain earlier than in adult patients. Reasons given for this include the possibility that children complain less than adults, and make fewer requests for treatment (Bush *et al*, 1989).

The main ways of administering drugs for acute pain are either through injection or pills. Injections of analgesics can take several forms. Some of these are **intravenous injections** of drugs such as morphine, for post-operative pain or a broken limb for example. Intensive care units often use intravenous drips of analgesics. The other method of giving intravenous painkillers is through **patient-controlled analgesia**. This involves the use of an infusion pump where the patient can press a button to administer a dose of the drug. The doses are regulated by amount and frequency to prevent overdose. Using patient-controlled analgesia avoids the delay in treatment of pain by busy ward staff, and can also give patients a greater sense of control over their pain.

Citron *et al* (1986) looked at the effects of patient-controlled analgesia on a group of male cancer patients with severe pain. Citron found that their rate of morphine use declined dramatically over a period of two days, when they were able to dose themselves.

Other forms of injection are nerve blocks and epidural and spinal blocks (caudals). These involve injecting local anaesthetic into the appropriate area – the epidural space in the spine in an epidural block, for example. Nerve blocks are commonly used for minor operations on hands and feet. Caudals and epidurals are used for the lower half of the body, such as in hernia repair operations or circumcision. Epidurals are used for Caesarean sections and to block pain in childbirth.

Commentary

There are particular problems with using drugs to treat chronic pain: addiction, tolerance and the possible side effects. Addiction should not be a concern if the appropriate drug is given for the appropriate pain, and if there is close communication between the person who prescribes and the patient. Citron et al (1986) note the possibility of overdose and abuse. However, the correct dose being pre-set, and a 'lockout' period (in which the patient cannot administer the drug) can control these problems. Tolerance can become a problem if increased doses of a particular drug are needed, although changes in medication can sometimes alleviate this problem. Long-term treatment can involve side effects of which the patient must be made aware.

In spite of these problems, medication is still commonly used for chronic pain, not least because if used correctly, it can bring real relief from pain. Types of medication used to treat chronic pain include analgesics that are used to treat mild to moderate muscle pain, for example, and anti-inflammatory drugs such as some steroids, which are useful for conditions such as arthritis and tendonitis.

Surgical methods

Surgical methods used to treat severe chronic pain are usually a last resort for both doctor and patient. Although surgery is considered to be a radical approach it can provide effective relief for very specific types of pain. Surgery is used, for example, in the treatment of **trigeminal neuralgia**. The problem with this type of treatment is that it can cause numbness in the face around the site of the nerve, and occasionally can cause paralysis. Another more successful treatment for pain is **synorectomy**, where the surgeon removes inflamed membranes in arthritic joints. However, despite the relative success of these procedures they are usually only used if all other methods have failed.

Commentary

Although they are not widely available, there are many other ways of helping patients control and manage their pain. Often sufferers of chronic pain need to learn to manage their pain, as many of the treatments available do not reduce the severity of the pain. In other words, the patients cannot control the pain completely, but can learn to live with it more easily.

Physical therapy for pain

There are two main ways of using physical methods to alleviate pain: **counter-irritation** such as TENS (transcutaneous electrical nerve stimulation), and **physiotherapy** or **massage**.

- **Counter-irritation:** here, TENS machines are used by placing electrodes on the skin where patients feel pain, then stimulating the area with a mild electric current. Although like acupuncture this method is used quite widely to treat chronic pain, like acupuncture, it is only useful for limited periods and is therefore more useful in the treatment of patients with pain that comes and goes. This way of controlling pain relates directly to Gate Control Theory, and the conditions that close the gate (see pages 64–5).

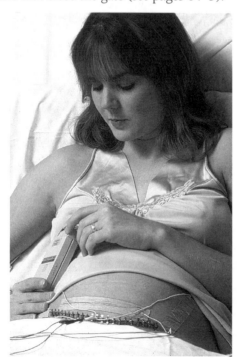

This woman is connected to a TENS machine, which is giving her mild electric currents to treat her labour pains.

- **Physiotherapy** and **massage:** physiotherapy involves the use of exercises to enhance stamina and relieve pain. A physiotherapist may set targets on a weekly basis for those who suffer chronic pain. Some pain responds well to physiotherapy – for example, the pain of arthritis is eased by keeping joints supple, and neck and back pain often responds well to physiotherapy and massage. Sometimes this kind of therapy does not relieve the pain, but because it can increase strength and stamina, patients can engage in more activity as a distraction from the pain, enhancing their self-efficacy and control.

Behavioural approaches to chronic pain

Operant conditioning

Pain behaviours are a sign that a person is in pain. Fordyce (1973) identifies operant pain behaviours that are conditioned to exist because of a number of different reinforcers such as attention from family and friends. People who suffer from chronic pain often learn to avoid activities that they have previously associated with an increase in their pain.

Operant conditioning attempts to remove the gains of sick-role behaviour by identifying and rewarding well behaviour. The two main aims of operant conditioning that follow on from this are to increase a patient's level of activity and reduce dependence on drugs (Turner and Chapman, 1982).

Bonica and Fordyce (1974) carried out a study on 36 patients using these techniques, and found the results were very encouraging. Patients had increased their levels of activity and decreased their intake of drugs. Operant conditioning programmes are often organized residentially, as there is a need to move the person from the environment that 'causes' the pain. Activity levels are increased by reinforcing behaviour with praise and families are taught how to encourage well behaviour (Fordyce, 1973).

An advantage of the operant approach is that it can be adapted for use with individuals of different ages and in different environments. Medication is usually given at fixed times using this approach and the dosage of drugs is reduced gradually. Studies have shown that the operant approach is effective in modifying people's reactions to the pain they are feeling.

Commentary

This method of treatment is not appropriate for everyone – for example, those whose relatives and friends are not very supportive cannot always use this method. People with progressive chronic pain cannot be helped using this technique. Another interesting problem in the use of this method is that some people may not want to engage in well behaviours – for example, those who are receiving some kind of benefit (such as disability payments, time off work and so on) for displaying sick-role behaviours.

Relaxation and biofeedback

Using this approach the muscle tension that is either the cause or effect of chronic pain can be reduced. Patients who learns **deep relaxation techniques** are generally more able to cope with their pain. Deep relaxation usually involves either contracting or relaxing groups of muscles systematically, or focusing on relaxing thoughts and controlled breathing.

Biofeedback, which monitors physiological function electronically through the use of EMG and EEG, enables patients to have a measure of control over what are otherwise unconscious functions. Patients use the readings to gain more control over their heart rates and breathing patterns.

Relaxation and biofeedback are used in various types of chronic pain relief, especially tension headaches and other stress-induced conditions.

Cognitive approaches to pain

Cognitive techniques used to alleviate chronic pain aim to alter the experience of pain by changing the way people who are in pain evaluate it. Through the use of redefinition, distraction and imagery, patients are taught to cope with chronic pain.

Redefinition

Redefinition is a process that involves a person replacing fearful or distressing thoughts about pain with more positive or realistic thoughts (Fernandez, 1986). Redefinition can occur in a number of ways. Explaining clearly what causes a chronic pain or giving accurate information about a procedure that has not yet taken place can help patients redefine how they feel about the experience when it happens. Reducing anxiety may reduce the expectation of pain and therefore the experience of it (Anderson and Masure, 1983). Using what are referred to as 'coping statements' is another way of redefining a chronic pain, where patients can tell themselves that they can cope, for example. Approaches such as this are similar to those for managing or controlling stress (see pages 83–5).

Many of the approaches used in pain clinics (see page 74) combine cognitive and behavioural approaches. Holroyd *et al* (1991) argue that combining these two methods of coping is a successful as drug therapy in reducing tension headaches.

Distraction

Distraction is a method where those in pain focus on a non-painful stimulus in their immediate environment. Doctors' treatment rooms often have pictures on the walls – especially for children – to distract attention away from any uncomfortable or painful procedure. Magazines and books also help to focus attention away from the cause of the visit. Beales (1979) described the use of distraction in a study that looked at how nurses distract children with conversation while a doctor is stitching a wound. Often children noticed no pain until the doctor commented on some aspect of the procedure, at which point Beales points out the children start to notice the pain.

Imagery

Patients can learn to use imagery by focusing on an image that is incompatible with or unrelated to the pain. This is sometimes referred to as **non-pain imagery** or **guided imagery** (Sarafino, 1994). An example of this might be a warm relaxing image, such as a beach or other place that the patient might enjoy. This technique is similar to distraction, since the person is distracting him or herself by imaging. Imagery works well with mild to moderate pain, rather than strong pain (Ralphs, 1993).

Commentary

- It is important that distraction is realistic and credible – asking someone to carry out a pointless task to distract his or her attention may not work. Something more meaningful, however, such as reading a book or watching a film might give more lasting relief. Similarly, a limitation of the use of imagery is how well a person is able to use his or her imagination – as some people are better than others at this technique.
- Cognitive approaches, such as **pain redefinition**, require patients to be articulate and willing to think and talk about their pain. This means that well-educated, middle-class people are likely to benefit more from this type of therapy than other people.

Psychotherapeutic approaches to pain

Therapeutic approaches can be used for those who suffer chronic pain that appears to have no physiological basis. Stress often appears to be a consequence of pain and, depending on the person, Therapy can help to reduce the stress, which in turn reduces the damaging effects of the pain (see the section on managing stress, page 83).

Insight-orientated therapy tends to be used if the chronic pain causes problems in interpersonal relationships. For example, the stress of having to give up a job and the resulting change of lifestyle can have far-reaching implications. The pain itself can cause a person to be irritable and perhaps less able to participate in daily tasks, and this can put great strain on relationships. Discussion in therapy sessions, especially those that involve patients and their families, can help all of them to understand the problems they experience in these relationships.

Improvements in family relationships can help to involve the family in treatment. Therapy is also often carried out in group sessions for the obvious benefits this can bring. Talking to other people with similar problems and experiences means that group members give each other social support.

Other treatments

Hypnosis

Hypnosis is not a widespread form of treatment for pain. Although it is gaining wider acceptability, it is still only a short-term treatment and relies heavily on a person's susceptibility to hypnosis. It is not clear what causes hypnosis to reduce the experience of pain, but Hilgard and Hilgard (1983; cited in Diamond and Coniman, 1991) suggest three possible uses of hypnosis in pain management:

- direct suggestion of pain reduction
- alteration of the experience of pain
- diversion of attention from the pain.

Hypnosis is, in fact, more widely used for acute pain and is gaining acceptance (though rarely used) instead of an anaesthetic. The use of hypnosis during surgery is not new. It dates back to the 1800s when cases of patients having operations and feeling no pain were recorded after they had been put in a hypnotic trance. However, the difficulty of being sure a patient is hypnotized and the difficulty associated with hypnosis means that it is not widely used today.

Placebos

The **placebo effect** is well documented as an effect that is not attributable to treatment, but the circumstances under which the treatment takes place (Payne and Walker, 1996). To 'treat' pain, a placebo is usually given in the form of a tablet (containing chalk or sugar) or an injection (containing saline solution).

A study that illustrates the effect a placebo can have is a study carried out by Gryll and Katahn (1978; cited in Kent and Dalgleish, 1996). In this study, dental patients were given a placebo pill before a pain-killing injection for a filling. In one condition, patients were told in a very enthusiastic way by the dentist that the pill was 'very effective in reducing tension, anxiety and sensitivity to pain'. In the other condition the dentist told the patients that 'this pill reduces tension, anxiety and sensitivity to some pain. Other people receive no benefits from it at all.' Those patients given the more enthusiastic message reported less pain from the injection and subsequent procedure than those in the second condition.

Pain clinics

Pain clinics have been developed specifically to treat chronic pain. Pain clinics focus on a multidisciplinary approach to the management and control of pain. Clinics use assessment and treatment methods that involve a number of different components – for example, drug therapy, physical treatments, psychotherapy, and cognitive and behavioural approaches. The aim of the pain clinics is to reduce a person's pain, improve his or her lifestyle, enhance social support and allow personal control (as Citron (1986) showed – see pages 71), and to reduce drug intake and the use of medical services.

Stress

Stress is one of the areas in which the interaction between psychology and health is most obvious. It is generally accepted that stress provides a clear example of how a person's mental state can affect his or her physical condition, and vice versa. This section begins by looking at different theories about the definitions and causes of stress, then goes on to describe the psychological and physiological effects of stress, different ways in which stress can be measured, and how stress can be controlled or managed.

Theories of stress

The 'fight or flight' response and the General Adaptation Syndrome

One of the earliest theories of stress was developed by Walter Cannon in the 1920s. He noticed that animals and human beings undergo certain physical changes when they are threatened and that these changes consist of **physiological arousal**. In other words, they have the effect of providing the organism with the physical resources to escape from the threatening situation, either by fighting the threat or by running away. These changes include:

- increased heart rate and breathing rate (to get more oxygen to the muscles and brain)
- improved blood clotting (in case of injury)
- dilation of pupils (to improve eyesight)
- hair stands on end (this makes cats, for example, look bigger and more frightening; in humans, this response manifests itself as goose-pimples).

In modern life, we are often presented with threatening situations that cannot be dealt with effectively by increased physical activity (this can happen when driving in traffic, for example). If the flight or fight response leads to increased physiological arousal, and this is not 'used up' by increased physical activity, it can leave one feeling 'edgy' (this process may partly account for road rage, for example). In the 1930s, Hans Selye extended Cannon's theory to include the physical harm caused by over-arousal (Monat and Lazarus, 1977). He developed a theory called the **General Adaptation Syndrome**, which has three stages:

1 **The alarm reaction:** this is the same as Cannon's fight or flight response. Selye found that the increased physical arousal that occurs during this stage is linked to the release of hormones by the endocrine system – a substance known as ACTH is released by the pituitary gland and this encourages the release of epinephrine, norepinephrine and cortisol by the adrenal glands. When these substances reach the bloodstream, the fight or flight responses are triggered. By undertaking experiments on rats, Selye concluded that organisms are incapable of maintaining a constant alarm reaction for lengthy periods of time; they die within hours. In order to survive, organisms enter a second stage – the stage of resistance.

2 **The stage of resistance:** here, the physiological arousal present during the alarm reaction is reversed to allow the body to recover, ready to face the next threat. However, even this process cannot be kept up for ever, leading to a third stage – the stage of exhaustion.

3 **The stage of exhaustion:** by now, the body is no longer able to recover from the alarm reaction. Selye describes it as 'at the end of a life under stress, this was a kind of premature ageing due to wear and tear' (Selye, 1977, p. 33).

Commentary

- Underlying Cannon's fight or flight theory is the concept of **evolution**. This theory suggests that genetic characteristics that facilitate survival are more likely to be passed on to future generations. In this case, organisms that are born with a weak fight or flight response are less likely to survive when threatened, and therefore less likely to reproduce. Animals with a strong fight or flight response are more likely to pass their genes on to future generations, so that, over time, the fight or flight response becomes strengthened.

- Cannon's fight or flight theory and Selye's General Adaptation Syndrome both define stress as an automatic physiological response to an external **stressor**. This is a **reductionist** approach as it ignores psychological and social factors. For example, not everyone shows the same level of physiological arousal when faced with a certain stressor; it is likely that an individual's cognitive response to a situation (what he or she *thinks* the probable outcome is) will affect the intensity of his or her stress response. Also, people often feel stressed even when they are not faced with an immediately threatening situation that would require a fight or flight response. Furthermore, it is possible to feel stress in the complete absence of any actual external stressor; if an individual *perceives* some kind of threat, then this is enough, and different people perceive threat to different degrees.

Cognitive conflict

There are several theories that describe stress as a psychological response, rather than a purely physiological one. For example, Heider (1946) developed **balance theory** in which he argues that people tend to organize the world into units and are motivated towards ensuring that these units exist in a state of **cognitive balance**. For example, consider a unit consisting of an individual, his or her doctor and a packet of cigarettes; if the individual respects the doctor's advice, and the doctor is saying the individual should throw the cigarettes away, but the individual wants to smoke them instead, then there is a lack of balance. In order to restore balance, the individual could change his or her attitude towards the doctor, or towards the cigarettes.

A similar theory is that of **cognitive dissonance** (Festinger, 1957), in which inconsistencies in a person's cognitions lead to an unpleasant psychological feeling, which in turn can motivate attitude change. For example, if an individual thinks he or she should give up smoking but does not do so, this will lead to the feeling of dissonance. The individual is motivated to reduce this unpleasant feeling by either changing their behaviour (that is, giving up smoking) or changing their attitude (that is, by convincing themselves that they do not really want to give up smoking after all, or at least not yet).

Both these theories describe stress as an unpleasant psychological feeling caused by inconsistencies or contradictions in a person's cognitions. Stress is a mental phenomenon, caused by contradictions occurring in the mind.

Commentary

- Why do human beings find mental contradictions uncomfortable? It may well be that our dislike of inconsistency has evolved, in the same way that we evolved a fight or flight response. If human beings did not find dissonance unpleasant, we would not be motivated to change our attitudes or behaviours in ways that may actually enhance our chances of survival.

- Theories of stress simply based on mental conflict add a psychological component missing from the theories described in the previous section, but they do not tell the whole story. For example, if a person is diagnosed as diabetic, he or she may feel worried about being able to cope with the illness; there is no immediate threat or alarm (so the fight or flight theory is an inadequate explanation of the person's feelings of stress) and there is no mental conflict (the person may be perfectly willing to follow the regime prescribed by the doctor, but still feel stressed).

Cognitive appraisal theory

This theory, developed by Richard Lazarus and his colleagues in the 1970s (Monat and Lazarus, 1977)

takes biological, psychological and social factors into account. Figure 4.4 illustrates the theory, which can be explained using the example mentioned above.

An **external stressor** could be a diagnosis of diabetes. **Primary appraisal** involves the individual in deciding whether the condition is a threat to his or her health. It is possible that the individual deploys ego defence mechanisms (see Chapter 1, pages 10–11) to persuade themselves that they are not really ill; in this case, the stressor is not perceived as a threat, and the individual will feel no stress (there are parallels here with the Health Belief Model and the Theory of Planned Behaviour (see Chapter 1, pages 11–15) – if an individual does not perceive a threat to their health, then they will not modify their behaviour).

However, if diabetes is perceived as threatening, the next stage is **secondary appraisal**, in which the individual evaluates whether he or she feels able to cope with the demands of the situation. Someone with a high level of self-efficacy and a strong internal locus of control is more likely to feel confident about this, in which case little stress will be experienced. However, if the individual is not very confident about his or her ability to cope with the demands of the situation, then that individual will experience the physiological and psychological responses associated with stress.

Commentary

Lazarus' cognitive appraisal theory adopts a **biopsychosocial** approach – that is, stress is not simply an automatic biological response or the consequence of mental processes, but arises out of the interaction between an individual's environment, his or her perception of threat and of the physical, psychological and social resources the individual able to deploy in order to deal with the threat.

Effects of stress

Apart from the immediate physiological arousal caused by stress, there are long-term health implications for people who suffer stress on a regular basis. A detailed discussion of these is beyond the scope of

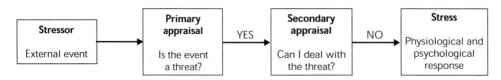

Figure 4.4: Cognitive appraisal theory

this book, but the range of diseases that have been linked to stress include:

- ulcers
- inflammatory bowel disease
- asthma
- chronic headache
- rheumatoid arthritis
- dysmenorrhea
- eczema
- hypertension
- coronary heart disease
- cancer.

Showing that a particular physical condition is actually caused, or made worse, by stress is very difficult as the majority of studies in this field are correlational (for example, see Key Study 7) – in other words, the studies show that people who are more stressed tend to be more likely to have, say, stomach ulcers, but do not demonstrate whether the stress causes the ulcers, whether people with ulcers are going to feel more stressed as a result, or whether there is a third factor that causes both the stress and the ulcers. The only clear way to prove causality is to carry out a controlled laboratory experiment, but it is clearly unethical to induce ulcers in human participants. However, experiments of this kind are undertaken on animals and, although it is difficult to generalize from animals to humans, a combination of correlational studies with humans and controlled laboratory experiments with animals convinces most people that there is a direct causal link between stress and certain illnesses.

The reason why stress leads to ill health in humans may have nothing to do with the actual physiology of stress; people drink more alcohol, smoke more, eat poorer diets and have more accidents when they are stressed. However, there is an increasingly large body of evidence to indicate that stress does indeed have a direct effect on health, perhaps by suppressing the immune system.

Psychoneuroimmunology is a relatively new discipline that is concerned with the effects that stress has on the immune system, and why it has these effects (see Bachen *et al*, 1997).

KEY STUDY 7

Researchers: Friedman and Rosenman (1959)

Aim: The researchers had previously carried out a survey of 'lay executives and physicians' who said that they believed that a major cause of coronary heart disease was excessive 'drive', competition, deadlines and economic frustration. This study tried to find a link between certain behaviour patterns and evidence of coronary heart disease.

Method: Three groups of men were used. **Group A** consisted of 83 men displaying a particular behaviour pattern, as follows:

1 An intense, sustained drive to achieve self-selected goals.
2 A strong competitive attitude.
3 A persistent desire for recognition and promotion.
4 Doing lots of things at once, constantly subject to deadlines.
5 Rushing physical and mental tasks.
6 Extraordinary mental and physical alertness.

These men were identified by colleagues at work and almost all of them agreed to take part in the study.

Group B also consisted of 83 men, businessmen or union officials, and were selected to match the group A sample in terms of age and physical characteristics, but to be exactly the opposite in terms of behaviour patterns.

Group C was made up of 46 unemployed blind men. These were chosen on the grounds that their visual impairments would lead to a lack of drive and ambition (like group B), but that they would exhibit a chronic state of insecurity and anxiety as a direct result of their disability.

The researchers carried out the following assessments for each participant:

- A personal interview about parental incidence of coronary heart disease, past and present illnesses, hours of work and sleep, smoking habits, physical activity and dietary habits. The participants' behaviour during the interviews was observed in order to confirm whether they really did belong in group A or group B (they did not do this for the group C participants because most of them displayed a 'general air of resignation, worry and hopelessness').
- A survey of dietary and alcohol ingestion.
- A cardiovascular survey: serum cholesterol levels, blood coagulation times, electrocardiogram readings and the incidence of arcus senilis were measured –these are all indications of possible coronary heart disease.

Results: As a result of the observations carried out during the personal interviews, 69 of the group A participants were judged by the researchers to display 'completely developed behaviour patterns', whereas this applied to only 58 of the group B participants. All of the group C participants seemed worried and apprehensive about the future. The results of the various measurements were as follows:

- Group A men worked more hours per week (51 hours on average) than group B (45 hours). Group C men were all unemployed.
- Group A men were significantly more active than group B, but not than group C; all three groups showed similar sleep patterns.
- There was no difference in the calorie intake or the amount of fat eaten between group A and B, although group C ate more than the other two groups.
- A greater proportion of group A men smoked cigarettes than the other two groups, and they also smoked more cigarettes a day on average.
- Group C men drank less alcohol than the other two groups.
- More group A men had a family history of coronary heart disease.
- On all the medical indicators of possible coronary heart disease, group A men seemed significantly more at risk than the other two groups (as much as five times more likely than group B).

Conclusions: Friedman and Rosenman concluded that men displaying certain behaviour patterns are more likely to contract coronary heart disease, but it is very important in a study of this kind to consider possible confounding variables. Some possible confounding variables can be eliminated at once, as there is no difference between the groups (sleep and diet). Others (exercise, tobacco, hours of work and alcohol) were eliminated because there was no correlation within each group between these factors and the risk of coronary heart disease. The fact that group A men were more likely to have a family history of coronary heart disease led Friedman and Rosenman to speculate that the behaviour patterns associated with groups A and B may be partly inherited. This last conclusion has led to psychologists thinking of these behaviour patterns as personality traits. In other words, people can either have a Type A or a Type B personality: Type A people are more likely to suffer from stress and therefore more likely to contract coronary heart disease. This study, then, is not just about whether stress causes heart disease, but whether stress itself arises from certain personality traits.

Commentary

Apart from leading to ill health, stress causes particular mental feelings and can also lead to changes in social behaviour. These kinds of reaction to stress are not always negative. The stress caused by a roller-coaster ride or by taking part in dangerous sports can, for some people, feel thrilling rather than unpleasantly frightening. Also, stress can be a motivating factor. The Yerkes-Dodson law states that given a particular task, there is an optimum level of stress that maximizes performance: too little stress and the individual is under-aroused and de-motivated; too much stress and anxiety levels get in the way of performance. (For a more detailed discussion of this see Legge and Harari, 2000.) However, most people usually experience stress as a negative mental phenomenon and would like to be less stressed than they are.

Psychosocial factors and stress

The conclusions of Key Study 7 suggest that being a type A or a type B personality may contribute to how stressed an individual gets, and that these personality traits may be partly hereditary. This represents a biological explanation of why some people get more stressed than others. In the following text, two psychological factors that contribute to an individual's stress levels are discussed (locus of control, and hardiness), as well as one social factor (social support).

Locus of control and stress

In Chapter 1 (see page 15) the concept of attributional style was discussed. A tendency to have an internal or external locus of control can make a difference to people's health-related behaviour. People who tend to attribute events internally are more likely to lead healthier lifestyles, but are they also less likely to suffer from stress? On the one hand, it

may be that feeling more responsible for what happens to you reduces stress as you feel more in control of your own destiny; on the other hand, perhaps the feelings of responsibility that accompany an internal locus of control cause greater stress.

A study carried out by Langer and Rodin (1976) attempted to discover the effects of giving people a greater sense of personal control. They compared two different wards in a nursing home for elderly people in Connecticut, USA. The residents in the two wards were of similar age, health and socioeconomic status, and they had been resident in the home for the same period of time on average (residents who were too uncommunicative or bedridden to take part were excluded from the study).

Both groups of residents were given a talk, but the issue of personal responsibility was strongly stressed with one of them and not the other. Furthermore, residents in this first group were offered a plant each for their rooms and were asked where they wanted it placed. Additionally, they were allowed to choose which night to go and watch a film. Residents in the other group were simply *given* the plant and *told* which night to go and see the film.

Even this fairly minimal manipulation of personal control seemed to have a dramatic effect. Residents who were given a greater sense of personal control were happier, more active, more alert and, when the researchers returned after eighteen months, were in better health and fewer had died. This study implies that having a greater sense of personal control actually helps to reduce stress.

Commentary

- There are methodological and ethical criticisms that can be made of Langer and Rodin's study. The sample was very limited (elderly Americans living in a particular care home). On the other hand, Langer and Rodin took care to avoid demand characteristics by not informing the residents, nurses or research assistants (who collected the data) of the purpose of the study. In the section on the effects of stress (see pages 76–7) it was pointed out that controlled experiments on the damaging effects of stress in human beings can be very unethical. In this case, Langer and Rodin would argue that they did not harm anyone's health, but actually improved it for those residents who were given a greater sense of control. On the other hand, when the experiment was over, we do not know whether the situation reverted to what it had been before, and it may be that being given a sense of control for three weeks, then having it removed again, did more harm than good in the long term.

- There are clear implications of this study for the way people are treated in residential homes. There is also a lesson to be learnt when developing therapy to help people suffering from extreme stress. If it is true that a low sense of personal control (that is, having a very external locus of control) can lead to stress, then in cases where this applies it may be beneficial for therapy to focus on shifting people's locus of control from external to internal.

Hardiness

Hardiness is a personality style described by Suzanne Kobasa (1979) that consists of three components.

- **Commitment:** people high in commitment involve themselves actively in whatever they are doing, being curious about and interested in activities, things and people.
- **Control:** people high in control believe and act as if they can influence the events taking place around them (that is, they have an internal locus of control).
- **Challenge:** this involves the belief that changes that occur in life are likely to be beneficial and lead to personal development, rather than seeing them as threatening.

Kobasa *et al* (1985) argue that the beliefs and tendencies that make up a hardy personality are very useful in coping with stressful events, whereas people with low levels of hardiness tend to find themselves and their environment boring, meaningless and threatening, and feel powerless in the face of stressors.

Kobasa demonstrated this by carrying out a study on 85 male business executives from Chicago, USA (chosen because of their stressful lives). For each participant, she measured their stressful life events, their hardiness (using a set of psychometric scales), the amount of exercise they took, how much social support they had (see below), and their physical and mental symptoms of illness. She found a strong relationship between hardiness, exercise and social support on the one hand, and illness on the other, but that, out of the three 'resistance resources' she studied, hardiness was by far the most effective in reducing illness. Kobasa concluded that people with a hardy personality are much better at coping with stress.

Commentary

It is easy to see why hardiness is helpful when it comes to dealing with stress, and this does have implications for treating stress. If it is possible to encourage people to become more hardy, then they will cope with their stress more effectively. The interesting question is what makes people more or less hardy in the first place? Hardiness is a personality style (that is, a tendency to behave in certain ways), and psychologists differ in their opinions about how people develop their personalities – in particular, whether personality traits are inherited or learnt. It is likely that hardy people are the way they are as a result of a combination of their genetic inheritance and their upbringing and environment.

Social support

Social support can be defined in two ways: first, by looking at the extent of a person's social network (family, friends, neighbours, community organizations and so on), and second, by determining the degree to which an individual feels that he or she has access to specific types of support, including:

- **emotional support:** people in whom one can confide in and share feelings with
- **instrumental support:** people who offer practical help, such as their time or money
- **informational support:** people who are able to offer useful information or advice
- **social companionship:** people with whom one can pursue recreational activities.

Whichever approach is adopted, there is a great deal of evidence that people with high levels of social support lead longer and healthier lives (Wills, 1997). However, it is less clear why social support should be so beneficial, and much research is currently being carried out in this area. Possible explanations listed by Wills are as follows.

- **Effect on physiological arousal:** there is evidence that the presence of a supportive companion actually reduces the fight or flight response, and consequently lowers subjective perceptions of stress and limits the harmful health consequences of arousal.
- **Effect on self-esteem:** people who perceive that there are others who care about them and to whom they can confide in tend to have higher levels of self-esteem. Also, the feeling that one is part of a larger community and accepted in a number of social roles may also increase self-esteem. It seems reasonable to assume that people

with a higher level of self-esteem will experience greater self-efficacy, and will feel more confident about coping with threats resulting from specific stressors – Lazarus' cognitive appraisal theory of stress (see page 76) predicts that such people will experience lower levels of stress.

- **Effect on depression/anxiety:** the perception that social support is available may make people perceive certain stressors as less threatening, thus decreasing their anxiety levels and increasing their ability to cope with stressful situations.
- **Effect on substance use:** people with high levels of social support drink and smoke less. This may be because such people are less stressed, or there may be a direct link between social support and substance use.

Measuring stress

There are two reasons why it is useful to be able to measure people's levels of stress: first, it may help with clinical diagnosis, and second, it is necessary for carrying out research into the causes and effects of stress, and the effectiveness of specific coping techniques. Referring back to Lazarus' model of stress (see page 76), stress can be assessed either by measuring the stressors themselves or by measuring the effects of stress.

One technique for assessing the stressors in an individual's life is to look at their social environment. Someone who is poor, the victim of harassment or discrimination, in a stressful job (for example, with long hours or that involves responsibility for other people's lives), or who has a difficult or disadvantaged home life is likely to be experiencing stress. However, this does not enable us to examine in detail the specific circumstances of a particular person. A more individualistic approach would be to ascertain how many actual stressful life events have taken place over a certain period of time. An alternative to looking at major life events is to assess the daily hassles that people are subjected to.

Measuring stress responses can be done by looking at the **physiological effects** of stress (either by measuring these directly, or asking people to report on their perception of how aroused they feel), **psychological effects** (by using self-report techniques to assess mood and attitudes) or **behavioural effects** (either by observing people's actual behaviour, or else asking them, or others, to report on it). The text that follows examines three of these tech-

niques – physiological measures of stress, life events and daily hassles – in more detail.

Physiological measures

The fight or flight response consists of increased physiological arousal triggered by hormonal changes. This leads to two different approaches to measuring stress physiologically:

- using blood or urine samples to measure hormone levels in the body
- using a **polygraph** to measure physiological arousal.

A polygraph is a machine that measures blood pressure, heart rate, respiration rate and galvanic skin response (that is, how much someone is sweating – this is done by passing a small electrical current across the surface of the skin and measuring the resistance).

Commentary

- The advantages of measuring stress in these ways are that they are reliable and objective (that is, difficult to falsify, either deliberately or unconsciously) and provide quantitative results (that is, numerical data, that can be used in statistical comparisons).
- The disadvantages are that they are expensive, requiring specialist equipment and trained personnel. Also, physiological arousal is not simply affected by stress. As described in the previous section pain can cause arousal, and an individual's level of arousal will be affected by other factors such as gender, weight, activity and consumption of substances. It is also feasible that having blood taken or being wired up to a polygraph machine actually causes stress in itself, detracting from the validity of these measurement techniques. Finally, if these physiological ways of measuring stress are valid, it is because they measure an alarm reaction. As argued above, it is possible to feel psychologically stressed without experiencing immediate changes in physiological arousal.

Life events

The previous section describes how physiological responses to stress could be measured. Another technique is to look at the causes of stress, rather than the effects, and the life events approach to measuring stress is based on the assumption that certain events in people's lives are going to cause them stress, and the more of these events occur, then the more stress there will be.

The earliest attempt to create a life events scale for measuring stress was by Holmes and Rahe (1967). They established their **Social Re-adjustment Rating Scale** (SRRS) by asking a large (but not particularly representative) sample to rate the degree of social re-adjustment required to adapt to 43 separate life events (such as 'death of a spouse', 'personal injury or illness', 'retirement' and so on). Items that were judged as requiring greater levels of re-adjustment were considered more stressful and had more points allocated to them (for example, 'divorce' was 73 points, 'son or daughter leaving home' was 29 points and so on). Individuals' levels of stress are measured by asking them to state how many life events have happened to them in the past 12 or 24 months, then the points for these items are added up.

Apart from the fact that the SRRS seems very outdated (for example, 'wife beginning or stopping work' scores 26 points) and ethnocentric (for example, 'Christmas' scores 12 points), it has some other major problems. For instance, items such as 'death of a close family member' are ambiguous as people may interpret the word 'close' differently (in fact, anxious people are more likely to feel that ambiguous life events have happened to them, creating a bias in the scale). Furthermore, the scale fails to take the meaning of the life event for the individual into account. 'Pregnancy', for instance, may be a very positive event for one individual and a personal disaster for another. And people may react differently to the 'death of a spouse' as a result of the nature of their relationship with their spouse, and also of their ability to deal with bereavement.

An attempt to overcome this last problem was built into a scale called the **Life Events and Difficulties Schedule** (see Harris, 1997). Without actually asking people about their subjective reactions to specific life events, this scale takes into account the likely meaning of each event for the person concerned on the basis of what most people with a similar background would feel. The interviewer uses a set of previously developed rules, based on extensive lists of precedents to translate the respondents' life events into a stress score (for example, 'pregnancy' would score much less for a married woman who already has a child than for a sixteen year old).

Harris quotes a great deal of empirical research that shows a correlation between high scores on the Life Events and Difficulties Schedule and a whole range of stress-related conditions, although is careful to say that life events on their own do not determine stress levels; rather stress arises out an interaction between life events, the meaning that those events have for individuals, and the individuals' psychosocial and physiological vulnerabilities.

Commentary

Although life events scales are cheaper than physiological measures (as they do not require specialized equipment), they are also less objective. Apart from the ambiguity mentioned above in deciding whether a life event has actually happened, these scales are vulnerable to falsification.

Daily hassles

Kanner et al (1981) challenged the life events approach to measuring stress arguing, first, that the correlation between life events and stress-related disease is not as strong as people claim, and second, that the irritating, frustrating and distressing demands arising out of everyday life are more closely linked to stress. They called these demands 'daily hassles' and developed a scale that measures stress by asking people to rate how irritating or annoying these hassles are to them.

Kanner et al also recognized that certain everyday events can have a positive effect on stress, and they called these daily uplifts. The Hassles Scale consists of a list of 117 hassles generated by the researchers (for example, 'misplacing and losing things', 'declining physical abilities', 'not enough time for the family', 'concerns about owing money', 'pollution'); similarly, the uplifts scale consists of 135 items (for example, 'being lucky', 'relating well with friends', 'getting a present', 'being complimented').

On both scales, respondents are asked to circle which items happened to them during the previous month, then rate each of these on a three-point scale relating to severity (for the hassles) and frequency (for the uplifts). Kanner et al claim that their hassles and uplifts scales are a much better way of measuring stress and therefore predicting stress-related illness than life events scales (see Key Study 8).

Commentary

Psychologists disagree about whether the life events approach or the daily hassles approach is the most valid way of measuring stress. Both techniques are currently used in practice. However, one advantage of life events scales is that they are slightly more objective; they simply ask the respondent to state whether specific events have occurred, whereas the daily hassles scale expects respondents to rate events according to severity.

KEY STUDY 8

Researchers: Kanner *et al* (1981)

Aim: To see whether the daily hassles and uplifts scales are more accurate in predicting stress than a life events scale.

Method: Some 100 participants (52 women, 48 men; all white, well-educated and comfortably well off) were selected from a population of 7000 previously identified for another study in Alameda County, USA. Each participant was assessed once a month for ten consecutive months using:

- a daily hassles and a daily uplifts scale developed by the researches
- a life events scale similar to the SRRS (Holmes and Rahe, 1967)
- the Hopkins Symptoms Checklist of psychological symptoms
- the Bradburn Morale Scale to measure psychological well-being.

Results: Kanner *et al* found that the hassles scale was a better predictor of psychological symptoms than the life events scores; when the effects of the life events scores were removed, the hassles score and the symptoms were still significantly correlated. The uplifts score was positively related to symptoms for women but not for men.

Conclusions: From this study it seems that daily hassles are a more valid way of measuring stress than life events. Interestingly, daily uplifts may be useful in measuring stress in women, but not in men.

Managing stress

This section describes several specific techniques for managing stress in the context of Lazarus' cognitive appraisal theory (see page 76). Figure 4.5 shows stress management techniques fit into this particular model of stress.

Environmental change

One way to prevent people from experiencing stress is to deal with the events and circumstances (that is, the stressors) that trigger the stress in the first place – for example, installing sound-proofing to eliminate noise pollution, breaking off a bad relationship, or deciding to stop taking part in dangerous activities.

One of the most powerful causes of stress in our society is economic deprivation, but as mentioned earlier in this book, tackling poverty is politically controversial. In many cases it is very difficult to remove the stressor, and impossible for the individual who is experiencing the stress. It is not useful, for example, to tell someone who is suffering from stress as a result of racial harassment to get rid of the stressor; that person cannot change his or her ethnicity, nor can that person single-handedly prevent other people from being racist.

Systematic desensitization

There are circumstances, however, in which an individual perceives a threat arising from a particular stressor, but this perception is somehow deluded or irrational. People with phobias or obsessive-compulsive disorders would fit into this category. For example, if a therapist has a client who is too anxious to leave his or her house, or has a phobia about a kind of everyday object such as balloons, it does not seem particularly helpful to attempt an environmental change aimed at removing the stressor. Rather, it would be better to alter the individual's perception of threat.

Systematic desensitization is a technique often used to help people with irrational fears. The patient is asked to relax and then presented with the anxiety-provoking stimuli at progressively more intense levels. Gradually, he or she stops associating the stimulus with anxiety or fear – and going out to the shops or balloons are no longer perceived as threatening.

Systematic desensitization is a behaviourist technique based on the principle of classical conditioning (see Chapter 1, page 8). A cognitive technique, in which the therapist explains to the patient that the anxiety-provoking stimulus is not actually threatening is unlikely to succeed, as most people with phobias already recognize that their fears are irrational.

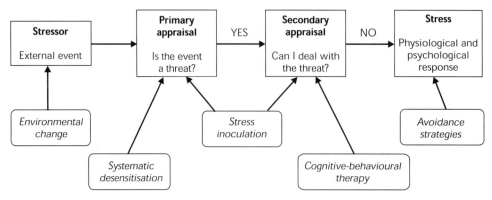

Figure 4.5: Specific stress management techniques

Stress inoculation

Meichenbaum (1985) adapted the process of systematic desensitization into a technique he called stress inoculation, in which people are exposed to stressful situations step-by-step, not only allowing them to get used to the situation and perceive it as less threatening, but also offering them an opportunity to develop specific coping skills and therefore to feel more confident about their ability to deal with the threat.

As participants are gradually introduced to the stressful situation, they are encouraged to express their thoughts and feelings through a series of self-statements. A child with a phobia about going to the dentist, for example, could be read stories about dentists and shown pictures before being taken for a first visit in which he or she would simply sit in the waiting room for a while. Eventually, the child could look into the treatment room, sit in the chair, become familiar with the instruments and so on, before treatment actually takes place. Specific coping skills relevant to this situation could include relaxation techniques in the waiting room or mental distraction during the treatment itself.

Cognitive-behavioural therapy

Cognitive-behavioural therapy focuses on the secondary appraisal stage of the cognitive appraisal theory of stress in that it has the dual aim of encouraging participants to be realistic about their ability to cope with specific stressors (that is, challenging negative thoughts), and also to actually improve that ability by developing appropriate skills and strategies.

This form of therapy is very commonly used to help people with anxiety and depression, and takes place in one-to-one therapy sessions, in group therapy, or even through self-help manuals. It incorporates a wide range of techniques which cannot all be explained in a book of this size (see Gilbert, 2000, and Fennell, 1999). However, they include the following:

- Getting participants to examine the evidence to support their thoughts and feelings (for example, 'Why do you think that nobody at school likes you?', 'What makes you think that you cannot write this essay – have you successfully written an essay like this in the past?').
- Considering alternative assumptions and conclusions (for example, 'Maybe your friend shouted at you because they are worried about something and not because they do not like you any more').
- Writing down the advantages and disadvantages of a particular course of action in order to help clarify conflicts and dilemmas (this is particularly appropriate in cases where the source of stress is a difficult decision that has to be made).
- Designing 'experiments' in order to test things out and rehearse new skills (this technique is similar to that of stress inoculation).
- Questioning self-critical thoughts in order to develop a higher sense of self-efficacy.

Avoidance strategies

All the stress management techniques described above are **problem focused** in that they involve dealing with the external and internal causes of stress. An alternative approach is to use **emotion-focused** techniques in order to minimize the negative effects of stress. At first glance, it seems obvious that the first of these approaches is likely to be more effective. Simply making oneself feel less stressed without tackling the stressors themselves (for example, by taking stress-relieving medication) seems to be a short-term solution only. However, there are situations in which emotion-focused techniques are more appropriate – for example, where the individual is powerless to do anything about the stressor, or where the levels of anxiety are so high that tackling the root cause of the stress seems impossible.

Physiological techniques for dealing with the effects of stress include physical relaxation, biofeedback and the use of recreational drugs. If an individual complains to his or her doctor of feeling overstressed, then there is a wide range of tranquillizers or anti-depressants that can be prescribed. Alternatively, people can use psychological avoidance techniques in order make themselves feel less stressed (see the section on ego defence mechanisms, pages 10–11).

RLA 9 shows how some of the techniques described above can be put into practice to help people suffering from too much stress.

- Distraction: here, the booklet describes techniques for suppressing unpleasant feelings by concentrating on other things, mental activity (for example, crosswords) and physical activity.
- Control of upsetting thoughts: by writing down 'anxious' thoughts, the aim is to 'catch' upsetting or frightening thoughts and to find a better way of thinking about the same things.
- Panic management: learning to recognize the onset of a panic attack and using a combination of breath control and modifying negative thoughts to control it.

Section 3 is about dealing with avoidance and loss of confidence, using a technique called 'graded practice'. This involves learning how to face difficult situations in easy stages, so that people can build up their confidence gradually.

Adapted from *Managing Anxiety*, by Dr Gillian Butler, Department of Psychology, University of Oxford, 1985.

Real Life Application 9:

Managing Anxiety

Managing Anxiety is the title of a self-help booklet aimed at helping people overcome anxiety and stress.

Section 1 explains what is meant by anxiety, and describes its causes and effects, stressing that anxiety is only a problem if it occurs at times when there is no real threat and when it interferes with everyday life. The booklet describes the dangers of avoiding stressors, arguing that the relief gained is only temporary and that the problem becomes harder to face in future. Interestingly, the booklet makes a point of stating that severe anxiety does not do any physical harm ('people do not die of fright'). This contradicts research that provides evidence of long-term health problems associated with stress, but it is important in a booklet such as this not to increase stress by making people already suffering from anxiety much more worried about getting ill.

Section 2 explains how to control the symptoms of anxiety by using a range of techniques, as follows.

- Relaxation: progressive muscle relaxation, relaxing thoughts and images, breath control to avoid hyperventilation, improving one's posture and trying to organize life so that it is less rushed.

Summary

- *Managing Anxiety* is a self-help booklet aimed at people who feel that their anxiety is irrational, or else so severe as to interfere with their everyday lives.
- It contains practical advice about a range of stress management techniques.

Questions

1 Is the general approach of Managing Anxiety problem focused or emotion focused?

2 Which of the specific stress management techniques described earlier in the text (see Figure 4.5, page 84) are referred to in this booklet?

3 The booklet actually misleads the reader in suggesting that high levels of anxiety do not cause health problems. Is this deception justified?

Chronic and terminal illnesses

The final section of this book examines a range of specific conditions that are chronic (that is, long term) and/or terminal (that is, life threatening). The symptoms and possible causes of these illness are described, and the psychological factors that can contribute to causes and treatments are discussed.

Asthma

The symptoms of asthma are periodic attacks involving shortness of breath, wheezing and coughing. Most asthma sufferers start experiencing symptoms between the ages of eight and twelve, and at least 10% of people suffer from the disease (about twice as many males as females). More children miss school because of asthma than any other illness, and the condition causes about 2000 deaths in the UK every year (Kaptein, 1997).

A typical asthma attack starts when the immune system reacts in an allergic manner and causes the body to produce a substance called histamine, which in turn causes the muscles in the airways to go into spasm. It seems that heredity has a fairly important part to play in determining whether an individual is likely to get asthma, but a history of respiratory infections is also influential.

Since the 1950s, asthma has been thought of by many health professionals and patients as a psychosomatic disease – in other words, one in which the symptoms are entirely brought on by psychological factors. In particular, as asthma occurs mostly in children, the symptoms were thought to represent a cry for attention from the mother.

Recent research seems to suggest that asthma is not caused by psychological factors at all, but this is still a fairly widely held belief among patients and doctors. One the psychological consequences of asthma is that patients and their parents sometimes feel anger, shame and betrayal following attacks, especially if appropriate preventive precautions have been taken (for example, keeping the home dust-free and using an inhaler).

These feelings represent the negative consequence of having an internal locus of control, which usually happens if people feel that the causes of a particular illness are purely psychological. People with an internal locus of control are more likely to take active precautions to prevent themselves from getting asthma, but if these precautions do not succeed, then people feel the guilt of failure.

Even if asthma is not psychosomatic, however, psychological factors are very important in determining how people cope with the condition. For example, two specific patterns of illness behaviour have been identified that are associated with patients taking more medication and needing more hospitalization:

- **avoidance:** people who use ego defence mechanisms to deny or ignore their symptoms of respiratory failure are less likely to take appropriate medication or preventive precautions.
- **panic-fear:** at the other extreme, people who overly focus on their symptoms are more likely to amplify them by hyperventilating (that is, rapid, shallow breathing) and to seek more treatment even though the symptoms are not objectively more severe than for other people with asthma.

Psychological treatments aimed at helping people with asthma include the following:

- **Reducing stress:** using techniques such as relaxation training, systematic desensitization and biofeedback. These approaches are aimed at helping patients cope with the symptoms of asthma attacks by keeping calm and relaxed (that is, by reducing the panic-fear element) and there is evidence to show that they are effective in enabling people to reduce medication levels in mild or moderate attacks (Sheridan and Radmacher, 1992).
- **Self-management:** self-management programmes seem to be effective in reducing the frequency and severity of asthma attacks in lowering rates of absenteeism and hospitalization, and in reducing the negative psychological consequences of asthma (Kaptein, 1997). In self-management training programmes, patients learn to recognize the onset of an asthma attack, how to avoid situations that are likely to provoke an attack, how to take appropriate action if an attack sets in, and how to cope with the social and psychological consequences of the illness.

Diabetes

Diabetes mellitus is a chronic disorder in which the pancreas is unable to produce enough insulin, a hormone that the body needs to digest sugar. About 2%–3% of the UK population are diagnosed with diabetes, with a similar percentage undiagnosed (Bradley, 1997).

People with Type 1 diabetes treat the disease by attempting to establish a balance between what they eat, the amount of exercise they take and insulin injections in order to maintain appropriate blood glucose levels, which is self-monitored using portable blood-testing kits.

However, the vast majority of diabetics have Type 2 diabetes, in which the pancreas has not completely failed. Insulin injections are unnecessary and the disease can be controlled through medication and diet alone. If blood glucose levels are not maintained, the patient suffers from **hypoglycaemia** (too little blood glucose) or hyperglycaemia (too much blood glucose). Both conditions can lead to other physical illnesses and psychological symptoms, and are potentially life-threatening.

The causes of diabetes are unclear, but, as for asthma, there seems to be an inherited susceptibility to the disease, and environmental factors that may have an impact are overeating and certain viral infections.

The key to coping with diabetes is constant monitoring of blood glucose levels combined with strict dietary control, other lifestyle management (for example, exercise), medication, and (for Type 1 diabetes) insulin injections. The importance of behaviour and the attitudes and feelings that underlie it means that health psychology has a large role to play in treating diabetes. Psychological factors that contribute to how people cope with diabetes include the following:

- **Personal control:** it is important for individuals with diabetes to have an internal locus of control as their behaviour is so critical to coping with the disease. As in the treatment of asthma, it is important for diabetes patients to recognize the onset of symptoms as early as possible, and to take appropriate action. Research quoted by Bradley (1997) indicates that some people with diabetes are remarkably accurate in recognizing blood glucose levels and that, although the physical and psychological symptoms associated with high and low blood glucose are idiosyncratic, they tend to be reliable in an individual, and that most patients, if not all, can be trained to recognize their blood glucose levels. However, controlling this disease is not straightforward. People who exert very tight control on their blood glucose levels suffer fewer medical complications (such as problems with eyesight) but are more likely to experience hypoglycaemia. A balance needs to be established between ensuring that blood glucose levels do not get too high and limiting the risk of hypoglycaemia. At the same time, it is important that medical targets are not achieved at the expense of psychological well-being. A tightly controlled lifestyle may lead to stable levels of

blood glucose, but may also make the patient miserable.

- **Avoidance:** non-compliance with treatment is a major factor in diabetes; Sarafino (1994) quotes research suggesting that 80% of patients administer their insulin injections unhygienically, 58% administer the wrong dose of insulin, 77% test or interpret their glucose levels incorrectly and 75% do not stick to their diets. The main reason for these high levels of non-compliance is that diabetes is actually a very difficult disease to cope with, but avoidance probably plays a significant role as well. Patients with diabetes may, for example, feel embarrassed about having to eat a special diet and needing food at very rigid times, or they may simply not like having to avoid food they enjoy (such as sweets and alcohol). The stress of having a disease with such serious health and lifestyle implications may be too much to cope with for some people. Finally, the long-term health complications associated with hyperglycaemia are easier to ignore than the short-term symptoms of hypoglycaemia, and there is a tendency for diabetes patients, and the parents of children with diabetes, to err on the side of high glucose levels.

- **Stress:** there is medical evidence that various stress-related hormones raise blood sugar levels and decrease insulin production as part of the fight or flight response, and therefore there is reason to believe that stress management would be helpful to diabetes patients. Evidence on the effectiveness of stress management has been mixed. In cases where blood glucose levels are tightly controlled, relaxation can actually make things worse. However, stress management is likely to be of benefit to people who have poor diabetes control, and who are experiencing stress, either as a direct result of their illness or in general. The greatest benefit will come to individuals whose lack of control is directly linked to their high stress levels.

- **'Psychosomatic families':** Minuchin *et al* (1975, cited in Sheridan and Radmacher, 1992) describe the characteristics of certain families in which failure to deal with psychological problems leads to failure to cope with diabetes, particularly in children. Psychosomatic families tend to have very close and intense interactions, with several family members becoming involved. They are

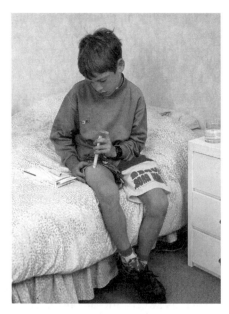

Regular insulin injections are vital for people with Type I diabetes.

over-protective of children and find it difficult to deal with changes. Finally, they tend to over-react to conflict situations and try to avoid them. Consequently, conflicts do not get resolved. Minuchin *et al* found that diabetic children in such families were very involved in the conflict between their parents, often siding with one against the other. By helping parents to deal with their own conflicts without using the child, Minuchin *et al* found that the adverse symptoms of diabetes in the child could be reduced.

Coronary heart disease

Coronary heart disease has already been mentioned several times in this book. Its high level of prevalence makes it a very important disease to consider (it is the leading cause of death in the UK, accounting for about 28% of the mortality rate). Coronary heart disease occurs when arterosclerosis (the hardening of arteries) affects the blood supply to the heart itself. This can lead to two different conditions: angina, which is an intense pain in the chest caused by insufficient blood supply to the heart, and myocardial infarction, or heart attack, in which the blockage of blood flow causes actual tissue damage to the heart muscles. Heart attacks are fatal in around 30% to 40% of cases.

Certain groups of people are much more at risk of getting coronary heart disease – men, people of lower social class, and people of Asian origin, for example. Heart disease is also linked to diet, smoking, (lack of) exercise and stressful lifestyles.

Clearly, some of these factors are not subject to change (for example, gender, ethnicity), but the fact that lifestyle and stress play such an important role in the onset of coronary heart disease, and that so many people get the disease, makes it a crucial area for health psychology. The ways in which psychology can help reduce the prevalence of coronary heart disease include the following:

- **Modifying Type A behaviour:** Friedman and Rosenman (1959; see Key Study 7, page 77) showed that a certain behaviour pattern, labelled Type A, was strongly linked to the coronary heart disease, at least in American men. There is evidence that Type A behaviour can be reduced using cognitive-behavioural therapy, and that this consequently reduces the risks of heart disease. Friedman *et al* (1986), for example, divided 600 heart attack patients into two equal groups. The experimental group received a range of cognitive-behavioural treatment, aimed at enabling them to alter their environment, behaviours and thoughts. The control group were given an equivalent time but this involved group meetings in which the problems associated with heart disease were discussed. After four years, the experimental group showed significantly fewer Type A behaviours but, more importantly, cardiovascular morbidity (that is, illness) and mortality (that is, death rate) were reduced by 50%, with a greater reduction for those whose Type A behaviour had been modified more.

- **Stress management:** stress, and in particular stress at work, has been linked to heart disease. If this is the case, then the stress management techniques described on pages 83–5 are likely to be effective in reducing the risk of getting the disease in the first place.

- **Promoting a healthier lifestyle:** smoking, exercise and diet are closely linked to coronary heart disease (Ogden, 1996). One-quarter of heart disease deaths are caused by tobacco, and smoking more than 20 cigarettes a day increases the chances of getting the disease threefold. A diet high in saturated fat resulting in high cholesterol levels can multiply the chances of contracting heart disease by three. Also, high blood pressure is a risk factor for heart disease, and this is affected by obesity, alcohol and salt consumption. Exercise that improves levels of cardiovascular fitness can reduce the chances of a fatal heart attack by 20%. Ways in which people can be encouraged to adopt healthier lifestyles are discussed in great detail earlier in this book.

Finally, people who suffer from coronary heart disease are likely to experience negative psychological consequences, and it may be possible to alleviate these. Bennett and Carroll (1997) describe how heart disease can have a devastating impact on patients. Its onset is sudden, painful and life threatening, and it causes high levels of anxiety and depression for sufferers. The worry of a heart attack can sometimes be too much too bear, and the avoidance that often results can prevent individuals from modifying their behaviour appropriately (for example, giving up smoking). It is likely that the chances of recovery for heart attack survivors can be increased by offering psychological treatments to help people cope with the trauma associated with the disease.

Cancer

Cancer, a disease feared by many people, is caused by the uncontrolled growth of abnormal cells, resulting in **tumours**. **Benign** tumours grow in one place in the body and are harmless in themselves; they can occasionally grow in places, such as the brain, and block essential functions but, once removed, they are unlikely to recur. **Malignant** tumours invade normal tissue; cancerous cells can break off them and be carried through the bloodstream or the lymphatic system to other parts of the body, where they develop into new tumours (this process is called **metastasis**). Cancer cells can originate in the tissue covering the internal and external surfaces of the body (known as **carcinomas** and accounting for about 90% of cancers), in connective tissue such as lymphatic vessels and nerves (known as **sarcomas** and accounting for 2% of cancers), or in the blood (known as **leukemias** and accounting for 8% of cancers).

After coronary heart disease, cancer is the second leading cause of death in the UK, accounting for about 24% of the mortality rate. For men, lung cancer is most common, followed by cancer of the colon and prostate; for women, breast cancer is the most common, followed by cancer of the colon, the ovaries and the cervix.

The role of psychology in the fight against cancer is similar to that for coronary heart disease. First, although there are genetic pre-dispositions towards cancer and some cancers are caused by environ-mental pollution, it is believed that many cancers are avoidable by modifying lifestyles. Second, cancer patients suffer many of the same psychological difficulties as heart patients, and they also have to deal with the unpleasant effects of cancer treatments. Furthermore, morbidity and mortality varies among people with the same type of cancer, and this may be due to psychological factors.

- **Lifestyle and stress:** as with coronary heart disease, both these factors affect the chances of contracting cancer. Smoking and diet, for example, have a very strong impact on cancer, and there is evidence that stress levels, stressful life events and different ways of coping with stress are also related to the disease (Ogden, 1996).

- **Personality/motivation:** it is commonly believed that a 'fighting spirit' is helpful in recovering from cancer and that patients who 'give in' to the disease are more likely to succumb to it. Eysenck (1988), for example, defines a cancer-prone personality as consisting of the tendency to react to stress with helplessness or hopelessness, and to suppress emotional reactions. These characteristics are not unlike those linked to hardiness (see page 80). If it is true that a certain personality, or motivational attitude, is linked to higher survival rates or decreased chances of getting cancer in the first place – and the evidence on this is fairly inconsistent – then psychologists have a role in encouraging people to adopt attitudes and approaches that are likely to be beneficial.

- **Mental illness:** cancer is linked to negative psychological symptoms in a number of ways. For a start, the cancer itself may damage the central nervous system, resulting in symptoms such as memory loss, confusion and disorientation, insomnia and so on. Brain tumours can lead to personality changes, affecting mood and behaviour. Cancer treatments, such as chemotherapy or radiotherapy, can also affect the central nervous system, resulting in symptoms such as hallucinations, anxiety, depression and sluggishness. One side effect of cancer therapy is temporary hair loss, and this can be very upsetting to patients. Finally, many cancer patients are forced to face the possibility of their own death, and this can cause psychological problems for the individual, as well as for his or her loved ones.

A final point to consider is the effects that potentially fatal diseases such as coronary heart disease or cancer can have on friends and family of the patient. For example, cancer patients who have been treated successfully are constantly on the look out for signs of the disease returning, and loved ones also have to live through this. They have to come to terms with the possible death of the patient and the fact that they may need care and attention. Additionally, cancer sufferers' families can sometimes find themselves in financial difficulties due to care costs and loss of earnings.

AIDS

AIDS stands for **acquired immune deficiency syndrome**, which is a condition almost certainly arising from a virus known as the **human immunodeficiency virus** (HIV). HIV attacks certain immune cells and, after a period in which no symptoms are apparent, the patient develops **AIDS-related complex** (ARC); the immune system is partially damaged so that patients become susceptible to all sorts of everyday infections. Eventually, the immune system is almost entirely disabled and the body becomes prone to opportunistic infections; these are diseases that are normally easily dealt with by the immune system, but are fatal in someone with AIDS. Patients do not die of the virus or of AIDS itself, but of the opportunistic infections that the body is unable to fight off. However, the virus itself does damage nerve tissue, resulting in neuropsychological impairment referred to as **AIDS dementia complex** (ADC).

The presence of the HIV virus can be detected in most body fluids but is only present in any concentration in blood and semen. Also, the virus is fragile when outside the human body so the only way it can be transmitted from one person to another is through direct interchange of blood or semen. This happens during unprotected sexual intercourse, when receiving blood transfusions that have not been treated, or when sharing intravenous needles without disinfecting them between one person and the next. These methods of transmission explain why AIDS patients tend to consist of people (both heterosexual and gay) who have unprotected sex with a lot of different partners, intravenous drug users and haemophiliacs (although the transmission of AIDS through blood transfusions has now been virtually eliminated). A small number of babies acquire the virus in the womb from infected mothers, and there have been a very few cases of health care workers accidentally becoming infected by contact with patients' blood. AIDS is more prevalent in certain countries where barrier methods of contraception are not easily available.

As with the diseases discussed above, health promotion is key in the fight against AIDS, as it is relatively easy to avoid getting the disease simply by modifying one's lifestyle. Psychologists also have a role in helping patients and their loved ones deal with the psychological difficulties associated with an unpleasant and life-threatening illness, as well as with the harmful side-effects of some of the medication that patients have to take. However, unlike the other diseases, AIDS has its own psychological and social issues.

When the disease first came to people's attention, most patients in the UK seemed to be gay men. Public attitudes towards the disease were affected by society's homophobia, and people with the disease became stigmatized and discriminated against. In terms of locus of control, AIDS patients, perhaps more than people with any other disease, were blamed for being ill. This environment provides the background to the specific psychosocial issues related to this disease.

- **Psychological problems** are common in people with HIV, but no more so than in people with other life-threatening diseases (Bor, 1997). People are particularly at risk when adjusting to a positive HIV test. Although cognitive-behavioural therapy seems very effective in helping people cope with the illness, there is nevertheless an increased risk of suicide in HIV patients. Even people without the disease can display psychological symptoms; some develop an exaggerated fear of contracting HIV and tend to avoid testing, or else are not reassured by negative tests. Others develop a delusional conviction that they have got AIDS, and seem to actually enjoy the medical attention. Not all patients diagnosed with AIDS develop psychological problems, but another contributing factor is that people with AIDS in the UK are more likely to belong to marginalized social groups.

- **Social problems**, on the other hand, are more acute for AIDS patients than for people with other diseases. The fact that people with AIDS are blamed for their illness, may lose their jobs, their accommodation or their friends because of the stigma associated with the disease, may be denied health care, or may be rejected by their families can cause real difficulties. Even the family themselves may suffer discrimination and, of course, announcing the onset of HIV could be accompanied by disclosures about lifestyle or behaviour that may be disapproved of. Keeping the nature of the illness secret could be a solution to these difficulties, but this has consequences for past and present sexual partners of the AIDS patient. People who refuse to undergo monitoring for heart disease or cancer are probably just being avoidant because they cannot face knowing that they have the disease. With HIV, another factor is that being tested HIV positive can have negative consequences of its own, even if the patient is displaying no symptoms. For example, it can be very hard to get life insurance, and therefore a mortgage, if you are HIV positive, and it is for this kind of reason that some people who feel that they may be at risk choose not to be tested.

Essay questions

1 Discuss the physiological and psychological causes and effects of stress.

2 Describe the different ways in which pain or stress can be measured and evaluate their effectiveness.

3 Discuss a range of different therapies/treatments for pain or stress and consider circumstances in which the different methods might be most appropriate.

4 Discuss psychological factors affecting people suffering from a specific illness.

# Advice on answering essay questions

Chapter 1

1 This question is asking you to consider specific examples of health-related behaviour (for example, alcohol use and exercise) and examine possible genetic and environmental influences. Genetic influences could include specific medical conditions, or inherited predispositions. Environmental influences include behaviourist learning theories, such as classical conditioning or social learning, and social influence, such as conformity.

2 This is asking you to describe the four cognitive theories described in the text (the Health Belief Model; the Theory of Planned Behaviour; locus of control; self-efficacy), to illustrate them with specific examples of health-related behaviour, and to evaluate them.

3 This essay asks you to consider ways in which cultural factors affect a person's health. You could describe genetic, social and environmental factors for each of your chosen cultural factors. You could evaluate these by using issues such as reductionism and generalisability.

Chapter 2

1 This question is asking you to repeat the exercise illustrated in RLA 3 (see page 31), but using another example of health promotion material.

2 For this question, you need to pick a health promotion issue (for example, smoking or use of condoms) and design a programme taking the theories described in the text into account. As well as referring to the Yale Model of Communication, you should also use the section in Chapter 1 entitled 'Improving health' (see pages 5–6).

3 In this essay you should look at issues relating to addiction – both physical and psychological, and behavioural explanations such as social learning. Other reasons for continued misuse include availability and acceptability.

4 In this essay you should look at examples of programmes aimed at preventing misuse (such as public health initiatives, workplace programmes and legislation) and those aimed at treating misuse (such as skills training, avoidance and the use of clinics).

5 Describe studies and theories that explain why people have accidents, and then look at ways of reducing these, based on appropriate health promotion campaigns that relate to the reasons for the accidents (such as the Yale Model of Communication, to provide information to overcome lack of awareness).

Chapter 3

1 In this essay you can consider the reasons why people do not adhere to doctors' requests, such as the complexity of the routine, rational non-adherence, relationships with doctors or perceived seriousness of the problem.

2 Patient–practitioner relationships can be affected by interpersonal skills, such as the interviewing techniques, and whether doctors are 'doctor' or 'patient' centred. There are also considerations such as non-verbal communication.

3 In this essay you can look at strategies to improve adherence, such as providing information and giving social support. There are also factors, such as the ease with which medicines can be used, and whether patients believe in their ability to manage the routine they have to adhere to.

Chapter 4

1 This question expects you to provide an overview of theories of stress (that is, the 'fight or flight' response, the General Adaptation Syndrome, cognitive conflict and cognitive appraisal theory) and also to outline the health related effects of stress.

2 Answer this question for either stress or pain. In

either case, outline the different measurement techniques described in the text. Evaluation issues could include their validity (that is, do they really measure stress/pain?), their cost and practicability, the theories of stress/pain on which they are based, how objective they are and so on.

3 Again, this question should be answered for either stress or pain. The text contains descriptions of several techniques for managing pain and stress. Describe them, then consider in which circumstances they may be appropriate to use (for example, avoidance techniques in coping with stress are useful if the individual is powerless to affect the stressor or else is so anxious that s/he needs to feel better before tackling the source of the stress directly.

4 Pick one of the conditions described in the text, and describe and evaluate the psychological issues associated with it. You could also suggest ways in which psychology can help people with the condition you are writing about.

A Advice on answering short answer questions

RLA 1

1 Epidemiology is the statistical study of disease. By investigating where and when cases of a particular disease come up, epidemiologists can develop hypotheses about causes, cures and influencing factors. This is different from medical research, which investigates the aetiology of disease – that is, the physical mechanisms by which the disease occurs.

2 Snow was unable to use medical science to deal with cholera as there was no known cure at the time; doctors were not even aware that cholera was caused by waterborne bacteria. He tried to encourage behavioural change by asking people not to use the Broad Street pump, but, when this failed, he resorted to a environmental 'improvement' – that is, taking the pump handle so that people could not drink the infected water.

3 This is a discussion point. On the one hand, Snow ignored the wishes of the people living near the Broad Street pump and imposed environmental change on them. On the other hand, by doing this he saved hundreds of lives. A major debate within health promotion is whether individuals should be allowed the freedom to harm themselves, or whether the state should intervene to protect them, even against their will.

RLA 2

1 The specific symptoms of anorexia nervosa are low body weight (less than 85% of the average), fear of weight gain, distorted body image and (for women) no menstruation for at least three months. People displaying some, but not all, of these symptoms, may well have some kind of eating disorder, but would not be diagnosed as anorexic.

2 Genetics: if anorexia is partially caused by hormone imbalances, for example, then drug ther-

apy may be effective. Behaviourist learning theory: behaviour modification could be used to reward people when they put on weight; with regard to social learning, it may prevent some women from becoming anorexic if there were fewer images of 'beautiful' thin women in the media. Social influence: school education programmes aimed at encouraging children to be more assertive and not so 'easily led' may be effective in reducing conformity. Emotional factors: if anorexia is linked to repressed fears and desires, then psychotherapy aimed at uncovering these unconscious thoughts may be effective. Cognitive theories: cognitive therapy that challenges people's beliefs and values may well lead to attitudes more conducive to healthy eating habits.

RLA 3

1 This question is asking you to take each sentence on the 'Sun know how' leaflet, and decide whether it is linked to any of the theories previously explained in the text. For example, the first bullet point under the heading 'Fact card' states that 'Skin cancer is the second most common cancer in the UK' – this relates to the Health Belief Model in that this sentence is attempting to increase perceived susceptibility. The last bullet point in this section states that 'Most cases of skin cancer could easily be prevented' – this is aimed at increasing people's sense of self-efficacy.

2 Discussion point: how and why do you think that this leaflet would be effective in modifying other people's behaviour, or your own?

RLA 4

1 The main problems that could occur if smoking is allowed in a university are litter, smell and passive smoking. Some would argue that allow-

ing smoking creates a negative image to outsiders and is immoral, because it condones a behaviour that is harmful to health.

2 A complete smoking ban will lead to smokers finding other places to smoke, usually around the entrances to buildings; this can lead to a concentration of smoking litter and environmental tobacco smoke, and to smokers gaining a higher profile and maybe even attracting sympathy.

3 Alternatives to a complete smoking ban could include segregated smoking areas, or some common areas in which smoking is permitted.

4 Discussion point: what do you think of the smoking policy at your college/workplace?

RLA 5

1 Discussion point: do you think nature or nurture is more influential? Can we ever know?

2 Other factors that might be important include imitation, depression and material deprivation.

RLA 6

1 Perceived seriousness and susceptibility (high) – benefits outweigh costs – likelihood of action (high).

2 A poster using the elements of the Yale Model of Communication.

3 No, because people can misrepresent what they actually do, as more objective measures show in this study.

RLA 7

1 Hospitals use these leaflets to reassure patients, and to give them clear instructions and advice about what to do and what to expect when they visit hospital.

2 Discussion point: some of the information is to ensure that the scan is as effective as possible – for example, how still the patient must remain. Other points are to reassure the patient – for example, about not feeling or seeing anything.

RLA 8

1 Congenital analgesia means that the person is insensitive to pain all the time (such as to heat or injury of any kind), whereas episodic analgesia is insensitivity to pain that happens in rare instances (such as after shock or trauma).

2 The strategies a person might use could be to have regular check ups at the doctor to check for trauma. A person could also use behavioural strategies of avoiding situations that could be harmful, such as tending fires or leaning on radiators. The person could also use cognitive strategies to remember to stretch often, and to check for cuts and bruises regularly.

RLA 9

1 Although *Managing Anxiety* does stress the dangers of avoiding stressors, most of the techniques described are emotion focused, in that they are aimed at helping the individual feel less stressed (using techniques such as relaxation and distraction). However, the booklet seems to be aimed at people suffering from quite high levels of anxiety, and so effective emotion-focused techniques may help an individual get into a frame of mind in which s/he feels able to tackle the problem directly, instead if panicking about it.

2 The booklet refers to:

- avoidance strategies, such as relaxation and distraction

- cognitive-behavioural techniques, such as controlling upsetting thoughts

- stress inoculation, referred to in the booklet as 'graded practice'

- environmental change, suggesting that one solution to stress is to organise one's life so that it is less rushed.

3 Discussion point: it may be useful to describe the harmful health effects of stress in order to encourage the perception of threat, but people reading this booklet have already decided that they wish to do something about their high levels of anxiety. Mentioning how harmful stress can be will only increase that anxiety, perhaps to levels that will undermine the individuals' attempts to tackle their stress.

R Selected References

Chapter 1

Ajzen, I (1991). 'The theory of planned behaviour.' *Organisation Behavior and Human Decision Processes*, 50, pp. 179–211.

Ajzen, I and Fishbein, M (1980). *Understanding attitudes and predicting social behavior*. Englewood Cliffs, NJ: Prentice-Hall.

Arber, S (1999). 'Gender.' In Gordon D, Shaw M, Dorling D and Davey Smith G (eds) *Inequalities in Health*. University of Bristol: The Policy Press.

Asch, SE (1956). 'Studies of independence and conformity: a minority of one against a unanimous majority.' *Psychological Monographs*, 70 (416).

Bandura, A (1965). 'Influence of models' reinforcement contingencies on the acquisition of imitative responses.' *Journal of Personality and Social Psychology*, 1 (6), pp. 589–95.

Bandura, A (1986). *Social foundations of thought and action: a social cognitive theory*. Englewood Cliffs, NJ: Prentice-Hall.

Bennett, P and Murphy, S (1997). *Psychology and health promotion*. Buckingham: Open University Press.

Blane, D (1999). 'Adults of working age (16/18 to 65 years).' In Gordon D, Shaw M, Dorling D and Davey Smith G (eds) *Inequalities in Health*. University of Bristol: The Policy Press.

Carroll, D, Davey Smith, G and Bennett, P (1997). 'Socioeconomic status and health.' In Baum, A, Newman, S, Weinman J, West, R and McManus, C (eds) *Cambridge Handbook of Psychology, Health and Medicine*. Cambridge: Cambridge University Press.

Drever, F and Whitehead, M (1997). *Health inequalities: Decennial supplement*. ONS Series DS, no. 15, London: The Stationery Office.

Elbourne, D, Oakley, A and Chalmers, I (1989). 'Social and psychological support during pregnancy.' In Chalmers I, Enkin M and Keirse M (eds) *Effective care in pregnancy and childbirth*, vol 1. Oxford: OUP.

Fletcher, A, Slogett, A and Breeze, E (1997). 'Socio-economic and demographic circumstances in middle-aged and older people and subsequent health outcomes.' *ONS Longitudinal Study Update*, vol 17, pp. 16–23.

Gil, KM, Keefe, FJ, Sampson, HA, McCaskill, CC, Rodin, J and Crisson, JE (1988). 'Direct observation of scratching behavior in children with atopic dermatitis.' *Behavior Therapy*, 19, pp. 213–27.

Hochbaum, GM (1958). *Public participation in medical screening programmes: a sociopsychological study* (Public Health Service Publication 572). US Government Washington DC: Printing Office.

Johnson, AM Wadsworth, J, Wellings, K and Field, J (1994). *Sexual attitudes and lifestyles*. London: Blackwell Scientific.

Khaw, K (1999). 'Inequalities in health: older people.' In Gordon D, Shaw M, Dorling D and Davey Smith G (eds) *Inequalities in Health*. University of Bristol: The Policy Press.

Law, C (1999). 'Mother, fetus, infant, child and family: socio-economic inequalities.' In Gordon D, Shaw M, Dorling D and Davey Smith G (eds) *Inequalities in Health*. University of Bristol: The Policy Press.

Naidoo, J and Wills, J (2000). *Health promotion: foundations for practice*. London: Baillière Tindall.

Nazroo, J (1999). 'Ethnic inequalities in health.' In Gordon D, Shaw M, Dorling D and Davey Smith G (eds) *Inequalities in Health*. University of Bristol: The Policy Press.

ONS (1997). *Living in Britain: Results from the General Household Survey 1995*. London: The Stationery Office.

Orbach, S (1978). *Fat is a feminist issue*. Feltham, Middlesex: Hamlyn Paperbacks.

Pelling, M (1978). *Cholera, fever and English medicine*. Oxford: Oxford University Press.

Pitts, M (1996). *The Psychology of Preventive Health*. London: Routledge.

Povey, R, Conner, M, Sparks, P, James, R and Shepherd, R (2000). 'Application of the Theory of

Planned Behaviour to two dietary behaviours: roles of perceived control and self-efficacy.' *British Journal of Health Psychology*, 5, pp. 121–39.

Ruble, DN (1977). 'Premenstrual symptoms: a reinterpretation.' *Science*, 197, pp. 291–2.

Schrijvers, CTM, Mackenbach, J, Lutz, JM, Quinn, MJ and Coleman, MP (1995). 'Deprivation and survival from breast cancer.' *British Journal of Cancer*, 72, pp. 738–43.

Seedhouse, D (1986). *Health: the Foundations for Achievement*. Chichester: John Wiley.

Senior, M and Vivash, B (1998). *Health and Illness*. London: Macmillan.

Sher, KJ (1991). *Children of alcoholics: a critical appraisal of theory and research*. Chicago: University of Chicago Press.

Strecher, VJ and Rosenstock, IM (1997). 'The health belief model.' In Baum, A, Newman, S, Weinman J, West, R and McManus, C (eds) *Cambridge Handbook of Psychology, Health and Medicine*. Cambridge: Cambridge University Press.

Sutton, S (1997). 'The theory of planned behaviour.' In Baum, A, Newman, S, Weinman J, West, R and McManus, C (eds) *Cambridge Handbook of Psychology, Health and Medicine*. Cambridge: Cambridge University Press.

Trowler, P (1996). *Investigating Health, Welfare and Poverty*. London: HarperCollins.

Ussher, J (1997). 'Gender issues and women's health.' In Baum, A, Newman, S, Weinman J, West, R and McManus, C (eds) *Cambridge Handbook of Psychology, Health and Medicine*. Cambridge: Cambridge University Press.

Wallston, KA, Wallston, BS and DeVellis, R (1978). 'Development of the Multidimensional Health Locus of Control (MHLC) Scales.' *Health Education Monographs*, 6 (2), pp. 160–70.

Wardle, J (1997). 'Anorexia nervosa and bulimia.' In Baum, A, Newman, S, Weinman J, West, R and McManus, C (eds) *Cambridge Handbook of Psychology, Health and Medicine*. Cambridge: Cambridge University Press.

Webster, R (1996). *Why Freud was wrong: sin, science and psychoanalysis*. London: HarperCollins.

West, P (1999). 'Youth.' In Gordon D, Shaw M, Dorling D and Davey Smith G (eds) *Inequalities in Health*. University of Bristol: The Policy Press.

Chapter 2

Banyard, P (1999). *Controversies in psychology*. London: Routledge.

Bennett, P and Murphy, S (1997). *Psychology and health promotion*. Buckingham: Open University Press.

Caplan, R (1993). 'The importance of social theory for health promotion: from description to reflexivity.' *Health Promotion International*, 8 (2), pp. 147–57.

Clayton, S (1991). 'Gender differences in psychosocial determinants of adolescent smoking.' *Journal of School Health*, 61, pp. 115–20.

Department of Health (1998). *Life begins at 40: health tips for men*. London: Department of Health.

Hartley, J (1994). *Designing instructional text*. London: Kogan Page.

Hill, JM and Trist, EL (1953). 'A consideration of industrial accidents as a means of withdrawal from the work situation.' *Human Relations*, 6, pp. 357–80.

Hovland, CI, Janis, IL and Kelley, HH (1953). *Communication and persuasion: psychological studies of opinion change*. New Haven: Yale University Press.

Jacquess and Finney (1994). 'Previous injuries and behavior problems predict children's injuries.' *Journal of Pediatric Psychology*, 19 (1), pp. 79–89.

Janis, IL and Feshbach, S (1953). 'Effects of fear-arousing communications.' *The Journal of Abnormal and Social Psychology*, 48 (1), pp. 78–92.

Lando, HA (1977). 'Successful treatment of smokers with a broad-spectrum behavioural approach.' *Journal of Consulting and Clinical Psychology*, 45, pp. 361–6.

Langley and Silva (1982). 'Childhood accidents: parents' attitudes to prevention.' *Australian Pediatric Journal*, 18, pp. 247–9.

Moolchan, ET, Ernst, M and Henningfield, JE (2000). 'A review of tobacco smoking in adolescents: Treatment Implications.' *Journal of the American Academy of Child and Adolescent Psychiatry*, 39 (6), June.

Naidoo, J and Wills, J (2000). *Health promotion: foundations for practice*. London: Baillière Tindall.

Oborne (1982). *Ergonomics at work*. Norwich: John Wiley and Sons.

Ogden, J (1986). *Health psychology: a textbook*. Buckingham: Open University Press.

Orford, J and Velleman, R (1991). 'The environmental intergenerational transmission of alcohol problems: a comparison of two hypotheses.' *British Journal of Medical Psychology*, 64, pp. 189–200.

Parry, O, Platt, S and Thomson, C (2000). 'Out of sight, out of mind: workplace smoking bans and the relocation of smoking at work.' *Health Promotion International*, 15 (2), pp. 125–33.

Pheasant, S (1991). *Ergonomics, Work and Health*. London: Macmillan Press.

Pitts, M (1996). *The Psychology of Preventive Health*. London: Routledge.

Rimm, EB, Giovannucci, EL, Willett, WC, Colditz, GA, Ascherio, A, Rosner, B and Stampfer, MJ (1991). 'Prospective study of alcohol consumption and risk of coronary heart disease.' *Lancet*, 338, pp. 464–8.

Roberts, G and Holly, J (1996). *Risk Management in Healthcare*. London: Witherby and Co.

Robinson, LA, Klesges, RC, Zbikowski, S and Galser, R (1997). 'Predictors of risk for different stages of adolescent smoking in a biracial sample.' *Journal of Consultative Clinical Psychology*, 65, pp. 653–62.

Rosenhan, DL and Seligman, MEP (1984). *Abnormal psychology*. New York: Norton.

Russell, MAH, Wilson, C, Taylor, C and Baker, CD (1979). 'Effect of general practitioners' advice against smoking.' *British Medical Journal*, 2, pp. 231–5.

Sarafino, EP (1994). *Health Psychology*. Chichester: John Wiley.

Sheridan, CL and Radmacher, SA (1992). *Health psychology: challenging the biomedical model*. New York: John Wiley.

Sayette, MA and Hufford, MR (1997). 'Alcohol abuse/acoholism.' In Baum, A, Newman, S, Weinman J, West, R and McManus, C (eds) *Cambridge Handbook of Psychology, Health and Medicine*. Cambridge: Cambridge University Press.

Wortel E, Degeus, GH, Kok, G and Vanwoerhum, C (1994). 'Injury control in pre-school children: a review of parental safety measures and the behavioural determinants.' *Health Education Research*, 9 (2), pp. 201–213.

Chapter 3

Batenburg, V and Gerritsma, J (1983). 'Medical interviewing: initial student problems.' *Medical Education*, 17, pp. 235–9.

Bourhis, RY, Roth, S and MacQueen, G (1989). 'Communication in the hospital setting: A survey of medical and everyday language use among patients, nurses and doctors.' *Social Science Medicine*, 28 (4), pp. 339–46.

Caldwell, JR, Cobb, S, Dowling, M and deJongh, D (1970). 'The dropout problem in hypertension therapy.' *Journal of Chronic Diseases*, 22, pp. 579–92.

Goffman, E (1971). *Asylums*. Harmondsworth: Penguin.

Hogbin, B and Fallowfield, LJ (1989). 'Getting it taped: the bad news consultation with cancer patients.' *British Journal of Hospital Medicine*, 41, pp. 330–33.

Kent, G and Dalgleish, M (1996). *Psychology and Medical Care*. London: Saunders.

Ley, P (1988). *Communicating with patients*. London: Chapman.

Ley, P (1997). 'Compliance among patients.' In Baum, A, Newman, S, Weinman J, West, R and McManus, C (eds) *Cambridge Handbook of Psychology, Health and Medicine*. Cambridge: Cambridge University Press.

Maguire, P and Rutter, D (1976). 'Training medical students to communicate.' In Bennett, AE (ed.) *Communication between Doctors and Patients*. Oxford: Oxford University Press.

Payne, S and Walker, J (1996). *Psychology for Nurses and the Caring Professions*. Buckingham: Open University Press.

Roter, D (1989). 'Which facets of communications have strong effects on outcome: a meta-analysis.' In Stewart M and Roter D (eds) *Communicating with medical patients*. Newbury Park: Sage.

Savage, R and Armstrong, D (1990). 'Effect of general practitioner's consulting style on patients' satisfaction: a controlled study.' *British Medical Journal*, 30, pp. 968–70.

Turk, DC and Meichenbaum, D (1991). 'Adherence to self-care regimes: the patient's perspective.' In Sweet JJ, Rosenskynad RH and Tovian SM (eds) *Handbook of clinical psychology in medical settings*. New York: Plenum.

Weinman, J (1997). 'Doctor–patient communication.' In Baum, A, Newman, S, Weinman J, West, R and McManus, C (eds) *Cambridge Handbook of Psychology, Health and Medicine*. Cambridge: Cambridge University Press.

Chapter 4

Anderson KO and Masur FT (1983). 'Psychological preparation for invasive medical and dental procedures.' *Journal of Behavioural Medicine*, 6, pp. 1–40.

Bachen, E, Cohen, S and Marsland, AL (1997). 'Psychoimmunology.' In Baum, A, Newman, S, Weinman J, West, R and McManus, C (eds) *Cambridge Handbook of Psychology, Health and Medicine.* Cambridge: Cambridge University Press.

Beales, JC (1979). 'The effect of attention and distraction on pain among children attending a hospital casualty department.' In Oborne DJ, Gruneberg, MM and Eiser, JR (eds) *Research in Psychology and Medicine*, vol 1. London: Academic Press.

Beecher, HK (1959). 'Relationship of significance of wound to pain experienced.' *Journal of the American Medical Association*, 161, pp. 1609–1613.

Bennett, P and Carroll, D (1997) 'Coronary heart disease'. In Baum, A, Newman, S, Weinman J, West, R and McManus, C (eds) *Cambridge Handbook of Psychology, Health and Medicine.* Cambridge: Cambridge University Press.

Bor, R (1997). 'AIDS.' In Baum, A, Newman, S, Weinman J, West, R and McManus, C (eds) *Cambridge Handbook of Psychology, Health and Medicine.* Cambridge: Cambridge University Press.

Bowsher, D (1993). 'Pain management in nursing.' In Carroll D and Bowsher D (eds) *Pain Management and Nursing Care.* Oxford: Butterworth-Heinemann.

Bradley, C (1997). 'Diabetes mellitus.' In Baum, A, Newman, S, Weinman J, West, R and McManus, C (eds) *Cambridge Handbook of Psychology, Health and Medicine.* Cambridge: Cambridge University Press.

Bush, J, Holmbeck, GN and Cockrell, JL (1989). 'Patterns of PRN analgesic drug administration in children following elective surgery.' *Journal of Pediatric Psychology*, 14, pp. 433–48.

Carlen, P Wall, PD, Nadvorna, H and Steinbach, T (1979). 'Phantom limbs and related phenomena in recent traumatic amputations.' *Neurology*, 28, pp. 211–17.

Carroll, D (1993a). 'Pain Assessment.' In Carroll D and Bowsher D (eds) *Pain Management and Nursing Care.* Oxford: Butterworth-Heinemann.

Carroll, D (1993b). 'Introduction.' In Carroll D and Bowsher D (eds) *Pain Management and Nursing Care.* Oxford: Butterworth-Heinemann.

Chapman, CR, Casey, KL, Dubner, R, Foley, KM,

Gracely, RH and Reading, A E (1985). 'Pain measurement: an overview.' Pain, 22, pp. 1–31.

Citron, M, Johnston-Early, A, Boyer, M, Krasnow, SH, Hood, M and Cohen, M (1986). 'Patient controlled analgesia for severe cancer pain.' *Archives of Internal Medicine*, 146, pp. 734–6.

Diamond AW and Coniman SW (1991). *The Management of Chronic Pain.* Oxford: Oxford University Press.

Eysenck, HJ (1988). 'Personality, stress and cancer: prediction and prophylaxis.' *British Journal of Medical Psychology*, 61, pp. 57–75.

Fennell, M (1999). *Overcoming low self-esteem.* London: Robinson Publishing.

Festinger, L (1957). *A theory of cognitive dissonance.* Evanston, Illinois: Row Peterson.

Fordyce, WE (1973). 'An operant conditioning method for the management of chronic pain.' *Postgraduate Medicine*, 53, pp. 141–51.

Fordyce, WE (1976). *Behavioural Methods for Chronic Pain and Illness.* St. Louis: Mosby.

Freidman, M and Rosenman, RH (1959). 'Association of specific overt behavior pattern with blood and cardiovascular findings.' *Journal of the American Medical Association.* 169 (12), pp. 1286–95.

Freidman, M, Thoresen, CD, Gill, JJ, Ulmer, D, Powell, LH, Price, VA, Brown, B, Thompson, L, Arbin, DD, Breall, WS, Bourg, E, Levy R and Dixon T (1986). 'Alteration of Type A behaviour and its effect on cardiac recurrences in post myocardial infarction patients: summary results of the recurrent coronary prevention project.' *American Heart Journal*, 112, pp. 653–65.

Gil, KM, Keefe, FJ, Sampson, HA, McCaskill, CC, Rodin, J and Crisson, JE (1988). 'Direct observation of scratching behavior in children with atopic dermatitis.' *Behavior Therapy*, 19, pp. 213–27.

Gilbert, P (2000). *Overcoming depression.* London: Robinson Publishing.

Gillmore, MR and Hill, CT (1981). 'Reactions to patients who complain of pain: effects of ambiguous diagnosis.' *Journal of Applied Social Psychology*, 11 (1), pp. 13–22.

Gryll, SL and Katahn, H (1978). 'Situational factors contributing to the placebo effect.' *Psychopharmacologica*, 57, pp. 253–61.

Harris, T (1997). 'Life events and health.' In Baum, A, Newman, S, Weinman J, West, R and McManus, C (eds) *Cambridge Handbook of Psychology, Health and Medicine*. Cambridge: Cambridge University Press.

Heider, F (1946). 'Attitudes and cognitive organisation.' *Journal of Personality*, 21, pp. 107–112.

Hilgard, ER and Hilgard, JR (1983). *Hypnosis in the Relief of Pain*. Los Altos, CA: Kaufmann.

Holmes, TH and Rahe, RH (1967). 'The social readjustment rating scale.' *Journal of Psychosomatic Research*, 11, pp. 213–18.

Holroyd, KA, Nash JM, Pingel, JD Cordingley, GE and Jerome, A, (1991). 'A comparison of pharmacological (amitriptyline) and nonpharmacological (cognitive-behavioural) therapies for chronic tension headaches.' *Journal of Consulting and Clinical Psychology*, 59, pp. 515–36.

Jensen, TS, Krebs, B, Neilsen, J and Rasmussen, P (1983). 'Phantom limb, phantom pain and stump pain in amputees during the first six months following limb amputation.' *Pain*, 17, pp. 243–56.

Jensen, MP and Karoly P (1992). 'Assessment of Pain Behaviors.' In Turk DC and Melzack, R (eds) *Handbook of Pain Assessment*. New York: The Guilford Press.

Kanner, AD, Coyne, JC, Schaefer, C and Lazarus, RS (1981). 'Comparison of two modes of stress measurement: daily hassles and uplifts versus major life events.' *Journal of Behavioral Medicine*, 4 (1), pp. 1–39.

Kaptein, AA (1997). 'Asthma.' In Baum, A, Newman, S, Weinman J, West, R and McManus, C (eds) *Cambridge Handbook of Psychology, Health and Medicine*. Cambridge: Cambridge University Press.

Karoly, P (1985). 'The assessment of pain: concepts and procedures.' In Karoly, P (ed.) *Measurement strategies in health psychology*. New York: Wiley.

Keefe, JF and Williams, DA (1992). 'Assessment of Pain Behaviors.' In Turk D C and Melzack, R (eds) *Handbook of Pain Assessment*. New York: The Guilford Press.

Kent, G and Dalgleish, M. (1993). *Psychology and Medical Care*. London: Saunders.

Kobasa, SC (1979). 'Stressful life events, personality and health: an inquiry into hardiness.' *Journal of Personality and Social Psychology*, 37, pp. 1–11.

Kobasa, SC, Maddi, SR, Puccetti, MC and Zola, MA (1985). 'Effectiveness of hardiness, exercise and social support as resources against illness.' *Journal of Psychosomatic Research*, 29 (5), pp. 525–33.

Langer, EJ and Rodin, J (1976). 'The effects of choice and enhanced personal responsibility for the aged: a field experiment in an institutional setting.' *Journal of Personality and Social Psychology*, 34, pp. 191–8.

Legge, K and Harari, P (2000). *Psychology and Education*. Oxford: Heinemann.

McGrath, PA and Brigham, MC (1992). 'The Assessment of Pain in Children and Adolescents.' In Turk DC and Melzack, R (eds), *Handbook of Pain Assessment*. New York: The Guilford Press.

Meichenbaum, D (1985). *Stress inoculation training*. New York: Pergamon Press.

Melzack, R (1975). 'The McGill Pain Questionnaire: major properties and scoring methods.' *Pain*, 1, pp. 277–99.

Melzack, R, Wall, PD and Ty, TC (1982). 'Acute pain in an emergency clinic: latency in the onset and descriptor patterns.' *Pain*, 14, pp. 33–43.

Melzack, R and Torgerson, WS (1971). 'On the language of pain.' *Anesthesiology*, 34, pp. 50–59.

Melzack, R and Wall, PD (1965). 'Pain mechanisms: a new theory.' *Science*, 150, pp. 971–9.

Melzack, R and Wall, PD (1996). *The Challenge of Pain*. London: Penguin.

Mersky H (1986). 'Classification of chronic pain: descriptions of chronic pain syndromes and definitions of pain terms.' *Pain*, Supplement 3, S1–S225.

Monat, A and Lazarus, RS (eds) (1977) *Stress and coping: an anthology*. New York: Columbia University Press.

Payne, S and Walker, J (1996). *Psychology for Nurses and the Caring Professions*. Buckingham: Open University Press.

Ralphs, J (1993). 'The cognitive behavioural treatment of chronic pain.' In Carroll D and Bowsher D (eds) *Pain Management and Nursing Care*. Oxford: Butterworth-Heinemann.

Richards, *et al* (1982). 'Assessing pain behaviour: the UAB Pain Behaviour Scale.' *Pain*, 14, pp. 393–8.

Rigge, M (1990). 'Pain.' *WHICH? Way to Health*, April, pp. 66–8.

Sarafino, EP (1994). *Health Psychology*. Chichester: John Wiley.

Selye, H (1977). 'Selections from the stress of life.' In Monat, A and Lazarus, RS (eds) *Stress and coping: an anthology*. New York: Columbia University Press.

Sheridan, CL and Radmacher, SA (1992). *Health*

psychology: challenging the biomedical model. New York: John Wiley.

Turk, DC, Meichenbaum, D and Genest, M (1983). *Pain and Behavioral Medicine: A Cognitive-Behavioral Perspective.* New York: The Guilford Press.

Turk, DC, Wack, JT and Kerns, RD (1985). 'An empirical examination of the "pain-behavior" construct.' *Journal of Behavioral Medicine*, 8 (2), pp. 119–30.

Turner, JA and Chapman, CR (1982). 'Psychological interventions for chronic pain. A critical review. 2.

Operant Conditioning, hypnosis, and Cognitive behavioural therapy.' *Pain*, 12, pp. 24–46.

Von Frey, M. (1895). *Untersuchungen Über die Sinnesfunctionen der Menschlichen Haut Erste Abhandlung: Druckempfindung und Schmerz.* Leipzig: Hirzel.

Wills, TA (1997). 'Social support and health.' In Baum, A, Newman, S, Weinman J, West, R and McManus, C (eds) *Cambridge Handbook of Psychology, Health and Medicine.* Cambridge: Cambridge University Press.

ⓘ Index

HEINEMANN THEMES IN PSYCHOLOGY

In-depth coverage of your A level topics

Approach your exams confidently

● Each book in the series gives you plenty of practice questions to develop your skills and help you take exams in your stride. Answers are provided too.

● Lots of real examples will bring psychology to life and help you work towards better grades.

Understand how to apply theory to real issues

● Each title shows you how theories are applied to current issues and includes suggestions for further reading to give you a wide understanding of the subject.

Learn how to use debates and studies to support your own arguments

● The books include key studies and encourage you to use these to support your own arguments. Summaries of opposing views in key debates are also included.

Order from your local bookshop using these numbers:

Memory	0 435 80652 1	Psychology and Health	0 435 80659 9
Psychology and Crime	0 435 80653 X	Psychology and Sport	0 435 80658 0
Psychology and Education	0 435 80655 6	Psychology and Organizations	0 435 80657 2
Clinical Psychology	0 435 80660 2	Human Relationships	0 435 80654 8

 **01865 888068**    **01865 314029**    **orders@heinemann.co.uk**   **www.heinemann.co.uk**

S 999 ADV 08

E641V

CARDONALD COLLEGE LIBRARY

3230017459